AN ORGANIC GUIDE TO LIVING HAPPIER & HEALTHIER.

WARDBODY:
IT'S A LIFESTYLE

AN ORGANIC GUIDE TO LIVING HAPPIER & HEALTHIER.

ANTOINE WARD JR.

An Organic Guide to Living Happier & Healthier
Copyright © 2018 by Antoine Ward Jr.

All characters and events in this paperback other than those clearly in the public domain, are fictitious and any resemblance to real persons, living or dead, is purely coincidental.

All rights reserved. No part of this publication may be reproduced, distributed, or transmitted in any form or by any means, including photocopying, recording, or other electronic or mechanical methods, without the prior written permission of the publisher, except in the case of brief quotations embodied in critical reviews and certain other noncommercial uses permitted by copyright law.

For permission requests, write to Antoine Ward. "Attention: Permissions Coordinator," at the address below.

Antoine@AntoineWard.com

AntoineWard.com

Quantity sales. Special discounts are available on quantity purchases by corporations, associations, and others. Orders by U.S. trade bookstores and wholesalers. For details, contact the publisher at the address above.

Editing by Patricia Waldygo
Designed by Antoine Ward

ISBN: 978-1-7337129-0-3
    Main category—Nonfiction›Self-Help
    Other category—Nonfiction›African American Gay Men

First Edition

Dedicated to the boy who constantly searched for a savior and soon realized he was it.

#selfmade

CONTENTS

Introduction: **The Philosophy of #WARDBODY**   11

Part One: **Rescue Yourself First!**   21
    Chapter 1: **Who I Am Not!**   23
    Chapter 2: **Do for Yourself, Always.**   45

Part Two: **Lead with Who You Are and Let the Rest Follow**   65
    Chapter 3: **It Will Always Start with You!**   67
    Chapter 4: **The Power of Going at It Alone.**   89

Part Three: **You're the Only One Standing in Your Way**   107
    Chapter 5: **Believe in You and Everything You Are!**   109
    Chapter 6: **Trip!**   127

Part Four: **Just Be Quiet Sometimes**   153
    Chapter 7: **A Glimpse of Enlightenment!**   155
    Chapter 8: **This Is WardBody!**   167

Acknowledgements   189
About the Author   193

"I was willing to completely die to any form of me that I had been, so that I could birth the woman I was becoming.... I hit my version of rock bottom, so I was willing to let go of everything and everybody.... I am much more valuable to my family and to my community because I was willing to let them go. Go through that door myself, teach myself, learn myself, condition myself, and then go back and get them. I am much more valuable to them now. But I had to go through a window time of ten years of judgment.... I had to be willing to allow my convictions to make me inconvenient. See we all want to grow, but we want to all stay liked by everybody. I was willing to be my own rescue at the risk of your approval."

– *Lisa Nichols, best-selling author and transformation coach*

Introduction
THE PHILOSOPHY OF #WARDBODY

What would your life situation look like when you become your own champion?

When trying to improve your life, undoing should be the first step you take—especially if you are someone like me. Someone who comes from dysfunction and grew up in toxicity. Undoing is an essential key to living happier and healthier. This process requires that you analyze your past—to help cope with, accept, or surrender to what has been. It requires that you get to know who you may have been, and who you are now. This process can expose so much of who you thought you were to who you actually are, that you may have not been aware of.

Allowing myself to go through the undoing process, I've been able to apologize, and fall in love with all of who I am and all of who I have been. This includes the broke me, the broken me, and dysfunctional parts of me. And because of this self-acceptance, I can now offer myself freedom to be exactly who I am. I understand that although I've been hurt, that doesn't mean I have to hurt others. Same with being lied to, and mistreated. I don't have to project what I've been through onto someone else. No one should have to, nor will they pay the price for my misfortunes. I now hold the keys to my new earth, and what looks like a spectacular future. I understand myself more. My likes, my dislikes, why I do what I do and why I react to things the way I do, both positive and negative. I made it my business to thoroughly work on myself, and by undoing I allowed myself to know that I am allowed to grow past what no longer stimulates me. Whether it's friends, family, life situations, or Traditions. I too can leave who no longer motivates me, or what no longer produces a certain quality in which I want to live.

I have not forgotten where I come from, for its where I come from that has drove me to where I am, and its what's going to push me to where I ultimately want to be. Undoing has allowed me to understand honest help doesn't come with a price tag and that some people may need you to play a role for them.

I am very grateful to have reached such an enlighten moment within my life because things could've been completely different.

1991: I am born on June 29 in Baltimore, Maryland, at Johns Hopkins Hospital on a Saturday morning at 10:05 AM.

1994: My father is sentenced to sixteen years in prison, and my life, as I know it, is about to change forever.

1996: My family and I are living on the west side of Baltimore, 3826 Park Heights and Keyworth. We have a pickup truck in the backyard that doubles as a playground, a Pitbull named

Wrinkles, and a cat named Pepper that I accidentally smother to death.

1998: I discover Saturday cartoons. *The Mighty Morphin' Power Rangers* comes across my screen, and I realize just what I want to be for the rest of my life: a hero.

1999: Life seems normal. My mom, my stepfather, my sister, and I all live under one roof. My sister and I share a room, but I am happy. I go to Malcolm X Elementary School, where I find out that I enjoy kissing boys.

2000: I attend Dr. Martin Luther King Elementary School. The kids can spot that I'm different, and they don't like it. I am being picked on a lot, surprisingly, by girls, and I don't know how to defend myself.

2002: My mother is sentenced to prison, where she will be for the next two years of my life. I now must move in with a play aunt who is physically abusing my sister, my brother, and me for everything under the sun. Also, her kids are A1 at bullying, as if slavery has made a comeback.

2004: My mother comes home, and we move into an apartment complex in McCulloh Homes Projects, 450 Watty Court. While I am happy to be out of the home of the woman who is abusing my siblings and me, I am very angry. But no one cares, and I don't know how to speak up to voice my thoughts and opinions.

2006: I am now attending Booker. T Washington Middle School, and at age fifteen, I have urges. I meet a guy named Douglas whose grandmother has an apartment on the floor beneath my family's, and he feels like home.

2008: I hate my life. I write in journals every day, asking, begging, and pleading for God to help me. My mother's boyfriend is abusive. My sister and I have both physically fought him, but my mother believes she is in love. So, he stays in our home; our home is not a home.

2010: My family and I face another eviction, our third one within the last two years, and I am tired of it. September of this year, I decide to move out and away from my family. I am eighteen and I just can't take it anymore.

2011: On April 29 at 6:00 AM, I get a phone call: my mother has been found nonresponsive. At 10:00 AM, my mom is pronounced deceased. I am nineteen years old, and aside from dealing with my personal issues, I now must take on the role of father. I feel completely lost. My life situation is too much for me, and I have no one to talk to, no one who understands. Help!

2013: My life doesn't belong to me. I feel depressed, and I'm very unhappy. I don't know what it means to live, to love, or to have fun. A close friend of mine tells me that if I want to move out of Baltimore City, I can do so. December 26, I move to New York City.

2015: My Life—My Life—My Life. My life finally feels like my life. I realize how much power is in my voice, and I learn to speak up for myself. I have taken control of my existence, and I am creating my new earth.

2016: My foundation is built. I have fallen in love with the broken parts of myself, my pain and my process. I understand why nothing in my life has been easy and everything makes sense now.

2018: I am the creator of WardBody, an active-lifestyle brand for the Everyday Athlete. I know just what I am doing, where I am going, and I know exactly who I want to be. My future is so bright!

So much has taken place in my life that I left out of this timeline, obviously. Yet I just couldn't give you everything up front. There'd be no reason for you to stick around to read the rest of this book, and I would like for you to stick around. But it's true: from ages twelve to twenty-three, I went from living what felt like hell on earth to a more meaningful, and purposeful life experience. After years of reflecting, I made a conscious decision to start falling into myself, meaning I began listening to myself, my feelings, my ideas, my intuitions, and my thoughts of *knowing*. I began accepting all that was and all that had been, and soon I was able to drop the victim that I identified with or that I wanted to be so badly because I felt life wasn't fair and/or if I was robed for my childhood and realized that I'd been chosen.

Further, I always knew I wanted to write a book. I plan to write four of them before my time expires here within this realm. Yet before doing so, I thought I needed either a PhD or a million dollars to get started. Who knew all you needed was a story to write a book? Although I am not that old, I like to believe I am a wise man. I feel I have learned the universal language and what it means (will explain what I mean by this) to be one with the way of the world. I have become pretty connected with the Universe; the Universe that not only you and I live in, but also the one that lives in us. Yes, that's right. I am the Universe, as are you.

This book is not a memoir. Instead, it is an accumulation of lessons I have learned from moments that took place in my life. These moments helped me define myself, what I am made of, and what it means to live a WardBody lifestyle. What you are about to witness in the chapters before you make up the foundation of WardBody.

Keep in mind that I have zero academic degrees or credentials in the art of telling others how to live their lives. I am not a life coach or a self-help guru; I do not claim to be an expert at living. What I do claim to be is a boy from the west side of Baltimore, Maryland, who was once a total misfit growing up in the projects of McCulloh Homes, who imagined himself to be a self-made individual. A boy who is working hard toward a goal in an unconventional way and has made something of the challenges and experiences that have come his way. A man who is ultimately looking to become an excellent being with a full, well-balanced, and meaningful life.

What Is WardBody, You Ask?

WardBody is an active-lifestyle brand for the Everyday Athlete, a brand whose mission it is to build a new earth by helping its consumer awaken his or her life's purpose through the power of self- and social awareness. We at WardBody believe that life truly tends to be lived once we understand what we are living for.

WardBody is an active-lifestyle brand for those who know they want to be great, those who want to live up to their own expectations of themselves, and those who actively get up every day, rise to every occasion, and get

THE PHILOSOPHY OF #WARDBODY

shit done. Essentially, putting in hard work when and where it's needed and pushing themselves past what they have defined as their *limits*. A wise man (Bill Bowerman) once said, "If you have a body, you are an athlete." Yet, while I have never played sports, this has not stopped me from training, thinking, or performing like the Athlete I know myself to be. Everyday Athletes consist of doers, such as the women behind xoNecole, or the squad that's running MEFeater Magazine. This also includes the young youtuber who is progressing with his content, the couple that started and maintaining their own production network. The women and men who sat out to work in PR, Marketing and Management that must fall a few times before they get it just right. These individuals are all studying, practicing, and getting better at their craft. They are all Everyday Athletes.

Whether in their professional or personal lives, they are achieving goals, preparing for playoffs—an actual playoff or a big client meeting that poses as a playoff. From new parents to social workers, these individuals are all planning and positioning themselves for what's to come or *the next play*. Some do it for belts and medals while others do it for titles and promotions. Some practice in physical gyms while conference rooms and classrooms may pose as others "gyms." The point is we are all training to become something or someone better, someone stronger, someone faster.

This guide is illustrated to offer you joy, both inside and out; let's call it *The Philosophy of WardBody*. It is all about self-reliance, self-love, and self-empowerment. It's a guide to a modern lifestyle, which I think should mean leading with who you genuinely are and letting the rest follow. It means coming to terms with the fact that you already have everything you seek. Not only do I wish to help you live a happier, healthier lifestyle, I hope to encourage you to recognize the collateral beauty in everything damaging

#WARDBODY

or broken. I want you to go, "OMG, if I hadn't gone through that, I wouldn't know this," or "I wouldn't be who I am today." Overall, I want you to know that there's no such thing as bad days, and there's no such thing as good ones either.

    This book is divided into four parts, with each chapter diving deep into my personal and professional life. I relay a lesson that I learned and explain how you can best apply that lesson to your life. I also include multiple journal entries I've written during my life. These sections are very important to me because they highlight some of the worst and best times I've experienced, from depression and hurt to discovering self-love and becoming enlightened. Please note, these journal entries range from 2010 – 2017 and are written exactly how they are in my Journal(s). Do not be alarmed of misspelling, word misused, and/or punctuation, I did this on purpose. This book will help teach you how to identify the unfortunate situations that may have unfolded in your life and use them as fuel to drive you for *Ward*. This book will also encourage you to grow past what was and into what is. It will teach you the importance of questioning everything that life and people in it have told you was *the truth* or *the right way*.

    Please note, the stories in this book are not laid out in any chronological order. Further, as you read and complete this book, I would like to you to hold on to these four pieces of advice:

1. Rescue yourself, first!
2. Lead with who you are and let the rest follow!
3. Never stop believing in yourself!
4. Just be quiet sometimes!

Got it? Great. Let's go!

Part One
RESCUE YOURSELF FIRST!

Chapter 1
WHO I AM NOT!

By a show of hands—yes, I'm talking to you—who here has been taught to identify who they are not? Has anyone encouraged you, or have you sought on your own to discover just who you weren't? Is it foreign to hear someone ask, "Who aren't you?" From a very young age, we're subconsciously programmed, in more ways than one, to find or define ourselves. What makes us, us? This then leads to a catastrophic web of confusion, sometimes guilt because the truth is not all of us know who we are, or we forget along our journey—which is okay. However, from the relationships we enter to the colleges we enroll into, the jobs we accept, and the religions we practice, life is divided up into ways for people to find out exactly who they are.

    We are forever looking to be found as if being lost in the first place doesn't benefit us more.

Growing up, I had a big imagination and an animated mind, yet, I was somehow overly shy. I was an uneasy kid, uneasy meaning very uncomfortable, with everything—myself included. Which caused me to spend a lot of my time alone. Uninterested in everything and everyone, I remember feeling I wanted nothing to do with the outside world. I felt like such a misfit within my family and a complete outcast in school. I was one of the few tallest guys in my middle school class and stuck out like a sore thumb. So that meant everyone saw me coming. One time, while attending Booker T. Washington Middle School, an administrator on my floor asked me, "Antoine, are you a loner?" Not knowing what a loner was, the uneasy kid in me became offended. "A loner?" It sounded like an insult. I immediately replied, "No," and quickly escaped the administrator's sight.

Due to my shyness, I never participated in any extracurricular activities or sought out to make lasting friendships. But somehow, that didn't stop people from being drawn to me. However, I prevented myself from experiencing so much because I was timid, and because I had huge trust issues. Today, as an adult, I can 100 percent tell you that I am a loner, and I am still very much so that same kid. A total misfit within his family and somewhat of an outcast within his peers. I've learned to be selective, yet, I'm still uncomfortable around large groups of people, and I remain to myself most of the time. The only difference is that as an adult, I own these things about myself.

On my *Soul-Searching* journey, I now understand just why I feel like an outcast within my family and my peer group. I realized my morals, priorities, and my ambitions are all completely different from my family's and the average twenty-something-year-old's. It's as if my dreams have made me an outcast. Personally speaking, no one in my family has ever gunned for something much larger in life, as I am doing. No one has set out to build something outside of themselves or their families. No one in my family, both blood relatives and play cousins, have voluntarily left those they loved behind to go off and make something of themselves, to chase a dream or to see just how great that are or could be. Also, no one else in my family, except me, is gay and has been forced out of what he thought was his comfort zone.

Now, I am not saying those apart of my family, both blood relatives or play cousins, do not wish to travel the world, want success, or want to see what their greatest is. Nor am I saying not being gay is the reason why they don't aspire to want more in life. Yet, what I am saying is no one that has been, or is a part of my family has tried to do these things—let's be honest, being the only gay individual, within a black household, comes with its own unique problems—and while all of this is okay, this is what, I feel, causes me to feel like an outcast from my loved ones—a great outcast but an outcast nonetheless. The things we get upset about, how we view life, it's all different, and as it should be. But as a young, aspiring entrepreneur, I don't strive for comfort, as my kin do. I strive for greatness, not necessarily wealth or money, but to see what I can handle, what makes me great? Which is unheard of within my family.

These days my family and I aren't seeing eye-to-eye on things. Yet, while my family is very supportive, I rarely talk about my dreams, or what I want to do in life. I tend to share surface-level things. However, given what I am doing has never been done, my loved ones don't fully understand what I must do, or the time needed to sacrifice, and the things I must go through, alone, to occupy the space of my dreams. Overall, I believe it won't happen until everyone can physically see the fruits of my labor to understand just why I don't travel home as much. So, for now, I'm viewed as the son who does not want to spend time with or is ashamed of his "ghetto family," or the brother who is selfish and doesn't care to provide for his siblings. Yet, I can accept all of this. I know who I am, and I am okay with it.

Further, the same goes for my peers. When writing this book, I lived in New York City, and as you know, or if you don't, this city is amped up 24 hours a day, 7 days a week. Yet like most introverts, before understanding, and accepting my true nature, I completely disregarded my introversion. To an extent, I had somewhat, hidden who I was from myself.

When I first moved to New York I assumed being part of a clique's and social circles and living it up meant I was doing my part at fitting in and enjoying my twenties—as "society" says we're supposed to. I created opportunities to be out and about, and before I knew it, I was part of *the scene*. New to the city and at war internally with who I was, I suffered through the social graces and "hung out," as was expected of me. While I felt honored to be in the presence of incredible people, I did not enjoy the nightlife lifestyle. It was not for me, and it was not me. Meeting up with the who's who and what's what every day or every weekend to brunch, mingle and gossip created an energy drain in my life; energy I soon took heed of and began listening to.

Through whom I thought I have helped me realize who I wasn't.

I grew to learn that my definition of fun and enjoyment did not consist of being slumped in a club, in my Sunday's best, trying my hardest to appear to a group of people who could care less about me. I was aware enough to know that I didn't want to spend my twenties running from my problems and searching for the answers at the bottom of a Rosé bottle or pretending to be someone I knew I was not. This lifestyle, this form of living, was not living to me.

Side Note: Here, I was writing from my perspective at twenty-two and twenty-three. Now at twenty-six, I've learned there are many different lifestyles you can CHOOSE to live in New York, or in general. Yet you must seek to live and experience life on your own terms—no matter where you live—or you will constantly live out the realities of those you befriend. You'll see and experience only what they experience. The word of the day is perspective—have your own.

The people in my life, at the time, didn't really seem to understand what it meant to be an introvert. Hell, I didn't fully understand what it meant. To me, there'd seem to be this notion that people who lived in New York, needed to go out every night to "Network." It's all I ever heard when I moved to the city. I soon learned that this is simply the NYC culture. Even my father, at times, would assume I was out networking or running amok when truth be told, I was more than likely home, lying across the sofa—watching Girlfriends or Noah's Arc—plotting on how I plan to shake things up. However, it was a process, learning how to accept who I wasn't and apply it to the lifestyle I wanted to live as a twenty-three-year-old, because, let's be honest, peer pressure is real.

Accepting these things about myself meant I had to undo what *was* and operate from a place of complete self-awareness.

I had to learn how to start giving emphatic "*Noes!*" and not soft "*Noes*," where you write "LOL" afterward because you don't want to hurt anyone's feelings. I had to start giving firm, direct, aggressive *Noes*! And to protect my introversion, I became less accessible.

It was challenging to do so considering my past. In the

past I'd I never set boundaries for myself or for others. As we urban folks say, I was with the shits. I allowed myself to get so invested in the lives of others that I'd find myself in situations that I was not proud of. Soon, when I started to speak up and voice—"No, I don't want to discuss that," "No, I don't want to be a part of that," "No, I don't feel like doing that"—it seemed as if I always had an attitude or that I no longer wanted to befriend those of who I was close to, which wasn't the case—until it was. I have lost a few friends living this way, but I now understand why. I've repeatedly been that person who has gone against himself to either be "a part of" or to be "there for" others and in return felt a lack of appreciation. I no longer cared to be *that person* and it was time for others around me to understand this.

Growing my sense of self, I began defining what things like self-love and self-respect looked like to me. No longer concerned with the superficial that's been my past; I felt there had to be more to life and I wanted to know just what that "more" was. Demanding that others speak to me in a certain way, not include me in discussions, and respect me—because I now, respected myself. I could feel this new version of self-made others uncomfortable simply because none of these boundaries were in place before. This is where feeling like an outcast came into play. While close friends and associates were with "the shits," I began taking a personal interest in understanding what mattered to me.

Know What You Don't Know

A piece of advice my father lent me, advice that I will never forget. I remember when he said it to me, I mumbled it back to myself: *Always know what I don't know?* When my dad gave me this gem, I wasn't vibrating at the frequency I am today, so I couldn't really comprehend what he was talking what he meant. I repeated it to myself again: *Always know what you don't know*—I held onto it.

Before offering me this advice, my father went on to express his love for how I choose to live my life, which came as a surprise because I was unaware as to how I was living. My father said to me, "Twan, man, I love how you live. You will try anything, no matter the cost or risk. You will give it all that you got, and if it does not work out, you will move on to what's next. I love that!"

I didn't know I was living in such a way. To me, I was doing what I had to do. But over time, my dad's advice and his compliment on how I lived my life came into fruition. I witnessed a moment where I sat back and said, to myself, *"Oh, this is what he meant by that."* From this, I learned it's only through what you don't know that you learn. When you are willing to admit you don't know, you're then aligned *to know*. From this piece of advice, I realized it's only through who you are not, comes who you are. So, who aren't you?

> The floor, walls, and the ceiling define the boundary of the room, but they are not the room either. So, what is the essence of the room? Space, of course, empty space. There would be no "room" without it. Since space is "nothing," we can say that what is not there is more important than what is there. So, become aware of the space that is all around you. Don't think about it. Feel it, as it were. Pay attention to nothing.

As Eckhart Tolle writes in his book, *The Power of Now*.

The idea of losing oneself occurs the moment adversity strikes. We are never found because we were never lost, to begin with. Constantly, you've been creating who you are—defining who you are—within the reality in which you live. Change a person reality, then what happens?

A man whose experienced humble begins soon hit it big. He no longer feels lost because he now has new opportunities, a new reality. Yet, to lose something means to have had "it" at some time before and either misplaced it, had it taken away, or cannot recover it. How does one lose what they never had? So, in all, it's only through whom you are not (being lost), and knowing what you don't, that you are taught.

So again, I ask, who aren't you?

From my dad's compliment on how I live my life, how I try something, give it my all, and move on if it doesn't work out. I learned that life experiences are designed to help reinvent ourselves. Life happens for us not to us, and those who suffer the most are those not willing to grasp this concept. Allowing yourself to let go of an identity that either you, your family, or your lover has emotionally, or spiritually placed upon you, grants you the opportunity for a lighter load. I like to think my father spotted this in me before I did. I have devoted my life to allow things (and people) to come and go, and like a stream of water, I am constantly willing to leave behind what's needed, which results in flow.

Holding yourself in a space where you are trying to be everything for everyone, is like committing mental and emotional suicide. The sooner you realize this, the sooner you can put an end to sabotaging self. You must be willing to accept and evolve or, in Christianity's teachings, you must be willing to surrender. The moment you say, "Universe (or God), I do not know XYZ," you're then given life situations to know that which you don't.

WHO I AM NOT!

Accepting who I *was not* had come during a time when I was trying so hard to prove to myself, and others, that I was either a great friend, an awesome brother, or a loyal guy to date, and it had all become too much. For example, I had two friends, one of whom I'd been closer to than the other. Still, I'd created relationships with both on separate occasions. These two friends of mine tried dating each other, and for whatever reason, things did not work out. To this day, I don't know why or what happened between the two of them.

As time went on, without any real confirmation, I could sense the two weren't seeing each other anymore. I could feel someone was off, and it seemed like some sort of tension brew between them. Soon, it was confirmed that they were, in fact, no longer dating and for one reason, or another, I thought it was my duty to make my friend's business my own. To be more specific, I thought it was my duty to make the business of the friend I was closer to—business my own because this is what real friends do, or so how I was raised to believe. My friend's beef became my beef.

Although I'd formed relationships with them both, I'd become closer to one, which made my decision to take sides seem "fair,"—but, in reality, it wasn't. The universe made sure to teach me a lesson for this. A few months later, I read a text between the guy I was dating at the time and this so-called friend, egging him on to sleep with locals on a birthday trip he would soon take. It felt like someone slapped me in the face. Yet, it was within this moment of whom I thought I was that opened me up to who I was not. I'd been operating as this ride-or-die person, only to discover that those I was riding with, or for, clearly did not feel the same way about me. More importantly what was taught, riding and dying for people was not real. You'll have friends that you mean more to than others, and not everyone has to be loyal to you, and those you are loyal too should not have a dictation over whom you can or can't befriend. A lesson we all must learn.

My role in friendships became so defined that I constantly found myself in situations that had nothing to do with me.

On another occasion, I recorded a guy—let's call him Mike—as he confessed to having a sexual fling with my friend's boyfriend. Interested in getting to know me, yet unaware of the relationship the person he was sleeping with was in, Mike wanted to be upfront and honest with me. He let me know he recently saw my friend's BF and me in photos together, and he assumed we were close friends. Doing what I now believe was the right thing to do, yet, not owning me any of this, Mike proceeded to be completely transparent in letting me know when, where, and how many times this "fling" occurred. Riding and ready to die, I had follow-up questions and as Mike answered, I recorded and sent the audio clips to the friend who this tea was about. But honestly, this had nothing to do with me.

Now, I know you reading this are saying, "But that was your friend, how can you say that?" Yes, and while this is true, according to my friend he knew what was going on within his relationship. Allegedly, this was not the first guy, nor the first time. So, I didn't need to go to such great lengths to provide him with this intel.

Shut thyen ass up!

I grew up thinking it was a must to insert myself in my friend's business or drama and that I owed the people I loved proof to how much I was there for them. I thought by

WHO I AM NOT!

putting myself in situations where I did not belong meant I was caring, and by supporting my friend's dysfunction and enabling their self-victimizing behavior meant I was doing my job at being a real friend, when in all honesty, I wasn't. Supporting a beef, or conflict of any kind is not something a true friend should expect from you and vice versa. A real friend would tell you to try your best at resolving whatever issue you may have, be it at work, in your personal life, or with your family.

I began feeling like I no longer wanted to be there for my loved ones anymore. I didn't want to have anyone's back or care, because I kept coming up short. Constantly jeopardizing myself and my well-being, and I felt shitty.

As I got older and a little wiser, I learned that when investing in any ship, friend or relation, or job, I become one with that person, place, or thing. Unaware, I never knew the emotional strain one could cause another by talking about how depressed or unhappy he or she is, repeatedly. That saying, "To the unhappy, it is a comfort to have had company in misery." is true. Understand that you have a choice. You can choose how much you are there for others I didn't know this before, it was either all or nothing. But now I know I have the option, I can choose whether, or not I want to allow myself to be consumed with someone else's drama. I can say, "I love you dearly, but I don't wish to be a part of this."

Further, I now understand for one to know who they are, one must know who they aren't.

Athlete's Tip: Moving forward, no matter how close you become or are to someone. You should not get in

33

the middle of situations. Remember: your mental health is everything. Come to accept, despite whomever you've known the longest and who gets along with whom, you have nothing to do with it. Be done with putting yourself in situations that have nothing to do with you. Also, note that you don't have to put others' happiness before your own, and, more important, you shouldn't have to.

Who They Say You Are

Before learning how to live for myself, I realized just how programmed I was. Subconsciously, and with the help of my parents, all I've known was to put others before by myself. If it wasn't my mother showing me through her failed attempts at relationships, and friendships, it was my father physically telling me I needed to stop being so self-centered or my siblings letting me know just how they felt about me when deciding to move out of Baltimore City to better myself. It had seemed with every attempt I made to live and experience life there was someone within my family upset with me about it.

Unlike my father, my mother never asked me to put others before myself. However, in more ways than plenty, she has shown me. I'd watch my mom go to such great lengths to care for people who could care less about her.

Love is what my mom had been searching for, and trying desperately to experiences it, she put not only herself in great danger but my sisters, my brother, and myself as well. There'd been a time where I physically fought a boy because he thought abusing my mom was okay, as did she, and I had to show them both that it wasn't. But my mother, like many others, mistook these acts of violence as love and continued to put up with and care for broken men. Which I believe made its way into my subconsciousness, and this behavior soon became me. I've never had a man put his

WHO I AM NOT!

hands on me, but I thought whenever I do date or sat out to get to know someone. It was my duty to look after and support toxic men or put up with some of the dumbest shit.

My mother and I continuously bumped heads over the men she dated. She thought she could fix them; she loved trying to heal broken men. I watched as she gave and gave—she gave so much of herself that in return she'd be left with nothing, literally. Evicted out of multiple homes, two of which happened because my mom thought it was a great idea to give our rent money to her guy friend(s) to flip. (I am going to assume you know what "flip" means.) Never going as planned, my family and I were forced to move. One year, our home was raided, due to an illegal substance being sold directly out of it. Soon, this resulted in yet another eviction and my mom having to spend Thanksgiving 2010 in jail.

My mother felt obligated to save whomever she could even if that meant making herself and her immediate family unhappy. Another time my mom agreed to let not only my best friend—at the time—live with us but also my best friend's mother, father, little sister, and little brother. Ten to a household in a five-bedroom home—it was the most uncomfortable situation ever! I was raised believing this type of support was normal, these acts of kindness are what garnet you a spot in heaven, or somehow bought you luck. For so long, I thought this is just what you do for people—repeatedly give, be there for, or try your best to save, and while these acts, in some cases, could be acts of kindness. You cannot save anyone if you (and your family) are barely getting by. This behavior has soon become me, and I found myself in the situations you've previously read, because of it.

My father never understood just why or how I'd become

so self-centered, and he hated it. I will discuss this more in chapter 2.

Aside from my mother unconsciously instilling in me that love meant sacrificing yourself to help others, my father did the other half of the work by telling me to do so. In 2018, I set aside some time to visit my family back in Baltimore. The night of my arrival, my father and I went out to have dinner and to catch up. I wanted to discuss a text my dad had sent to me a few days prior to my arrival. The text read, "Being a man is a thankless job. As a brother, a father, or a husband, you have to give and not expect nothing in return." It was this message, or piece of advice this advice that I lived by, that caused me to suffer in silence for four years of my life.

When I was nineteen, my mother passed away from thyroid cancer, and because I am the oldest, I became the decision maker for everything. Overnight, I went from being a son, dealing with his sexuality and personal issues, to a father of three, with a fourth one on the way; my sister was due that July. Although I'd felt I never had a childhood when my mom passed, the entire course of my life changed, and a new level of maturity was upon me. At nineteen, it was my duty to make sure my mom had a proper farewell. This meant, for starters, I had to raise $5000 for the funeral, pick out flowers, a casket, and the clothes she'd be wearing. I too had to write the obituary and sit down with the funeral director to let him know that I could only afford to cremate my mother, instead of burying her. With my world upside down, all I wanted was to be left alone.

For me, there was no time to mourn. I had to shoulder

the responsibility and make things happen and make sure my siblings understood things were going to be all right—when in fact I didn't know if they were. Thinking back, I felt left out. There was not a care insight when it came to me, and I am sure this is what my father meant when he said being a man is a thankless job because in my case it seemed to be.

Years after the death of my mom, I felt very much alone, but I knew not to turn to anything outside of myself to help cope. Coming from a long line of addicts, I knew not to use drugs or abuse alcohol, given my family's history. My grandmother (mother's mom) was an alcoholic and passed away from it and watching my grandfather (mother's dad) sit at the dining room table high, nodding, as he tries to help my sister and me with our homework. My father side of the family was the same. I also knew I didn't want to turn to men to feel better or use sex to fill the voids that were me. For as long as I could remember I have always tried to prioritize what mattered more.

Moreover, I never for a second, contemplated taking my life. Although this time had become stressful, I never thought twice about not rising to the occasion. There was a ton on my plate, and I had no one to confide in, no one, I felt, to help lighten my load.

However, even though this moment, this time in my life, was so stressful. I knew this was such a defining moment, and I knew from then on, no matter where I go, whom I lost, what I go through, I would be all right.

Further, I dealt with this sense of being alone or loneliness until I was about twenty-three; and the depression that came along with it. It felt I was struggling with trying to live for myself, instead of dealing with the loss of my mom. I wanted to be better, for myself, but I didn't know how to. I'd been playing the role of a caretaker, and I didn't know how to care for myself.

That year, I wasn't going to celebrate Christmas or any holiday, for that matter, but I wanted my siblings' first Christmas without our mother to be spent together. I'd maxed out both of my credit cards so everyone could have gifts. Though instead, on the actual day of Christmas, my siblings all had different plans. So, I saw no one, and because I was so invested in my role as a father/brother that I was playing, I couldn't help but feel like my kids were now grown and did not have time to spend with me—It was so weird. The same went for when my niece came into this world. Because my sister and our father did not see eye-to-eye (nor had they ever), this made me Brother, Dad, Grandpa, and Uncle Antoine all at the same time.

All these things were things I thought about when my father stated, "Being a man is a thankless job," because in my case it was the truth. No one had thanked me for the sacrifices I'd made to be there for them—not that anyone owed me that, but it would've been great to hear given I was twenty-one and didn't know whether I was coming or going, or if I was doing a great job. Instead, when I wasn't available or tried doing my own thing, *"You can die slow. " "Man, F*&% you." "You can catch aids for all I care."* was all I heard from my siblings. Not one Thank you, even till this day, but it's okay.

More so, I'd been all these things to other people, but not once did I know how to be any of those things for myself.

Now that I am older and able to comprehend "people will only do what you allow." I understand that being a man will only be a thankless job if I allow it to be. My dad misused his words when telling me what he did. However, as a son, boyfriend, husband, or brother, I require appreciation, love, and respect and I will not accept or tolerate anything less.

> *Athlete's Tip:* Note that you tell people who you are and what you're about in the way you answer to them. You do not have to be what they say you are. You have a choice. There will be times when others will try their best to attack you because you aren't willing to star in the role that they need you to play. You will be called things like selfish, stingy, self-centered, and so on. However, know that you have an overall say about who you are in the end. People can describe you or how they see you, but no one can tell you who you are or aren't. You shouldn't have to play roles to make people feel as if they are who they are. You can live your life the way you see fit, for you.

Wanting more is okay. You should not feel guilty about this. Anyone who truly loves and cares about you would not ask you to sacrifice or compromise yourself for their wants or needs. Also, know that It's okay to leave where you are when you feel where you are no longer offers you what you want.

Constant Dysfunction

Making the permanent decision to move out of my birth state, I made it my mission to be more open to new experiences and possibilities. This was a significant change for me, coming from the ghetto. Before relocating to NYC, I didn't have a chance to live life in a way I saw fit. I couldn't live comfortably as an openly gay man—yes, that's right, I am gay. Living in Baltimore—when I did, where I did—

being gay wasn't "it." Again, I had to hide the true nature of who I was to protect myself; this meant trying to walk "straighter," act straighter and disguise my tone to sound hetero. Reminded with every word I spoke, it's been told to put some bass in my voice. Which I have always been a little insecure about because my voice is not naturally deep. Which then made me not want to talk altogether because I was afraid that people would hear the femininity in it. However, when I moved to NYC, all bets were off. **#YAS**. I'd given myself a fresh start, and by moving to one of the gayest cities on earth, I was about to learn just how vital having a voice was.

Settling into the new chapter that was now my life, I was part of a new set of friends, and within this circle of friends It seemed that everyone had a prominent personality. It was like we were all auditioning to hold a peach on *The Real Housewives of Atlanta*. I mean, we would shade one another for no apparent reason, and we would go in. We slandered each other using sensitive information that another person had told us, in confidence, and threw it back in one another's face. Looking back, I recognize that these friendships were so toxic, but toxic was all I ever knew. All my life, I've known only of dysfunction, and because of this, these friends felt like home.

    I had become a product of my environment, as we all are at some point within our lives, but it didn't take long before I cut everyone off and went my separate way. However, before getting to that point, I witnessed my internal-self trying to tell my external-self to break away, and to remove myself from this circle. When occupying this space my energy was dull, and my vibrations were low. We would gossip, discussing other's business versus the plans to elevate ourselves. I felt unproductive in every aspect of my life, and while my intuition of knowing what needed to be done haunted my gut, I ignored it. I now know that when this happens, I need to remove either myself or others from my life situation.

> **Side Note: Pay attention to where your energy and vibrations drop and who you are around when it does. Whether you're at work, or when you are among a particular set of people, or even in your relationship. Your inner and outer selves are having conversations, and you should do yourself a favor and listen up. It's like you always know what you need to do. Please do not ignore it.**

Though, because I suppressed this inner voice telling me to leave, the dysfunction continued. In this group, there'd been a guy I never really considered to be an actual friend. He was more of an associate, which means our ties with one another were not strong. We did not owe each other anything, and it was what it was, at least for me. For his twenty-seventh birthday, he invited everyone, me included, on a seven-day cruise to help celebrate. I played this incident back in my head a few times, asking "Why did I even agree to go in the first place?" However, I agreed. The associate and I had a mutual friend, and I'd mentioned to her I didn't want to go, but because he'd invited me, I guessed I would. Later that week, we all sat around discussing the details of, and plans for, this trip, and the associate's and I mutual friend good friend told him that she was not spending forty-eight days–**#SHADE**–at sea with him and his family. Birthday boy-to-be Kanye Shrugged and moved on. "Okay," he replied. Again, because this group was so dysfunctional, our mutual friend made it her business to yell out, "Well, Antoine doesn't want to go either!"

However, in my defense, the reason was due to my finances. I'd just paid for a trip I was taking that December, and to settle for another one in August was pushing it. Then, on top of that, I was making only $8.75 an hour at my job. Had the associate tried to find this out, he would've known this was why I didn't—better yet, I couldn't go.

I grew upset with myself because had I been able to say, "Thank you, but no thank you," when the invitation came my way, I would've saved myself a lot of time and energy. So, by not listening to my intuition, I caused myself unnecessary drama. Not for nothing, you would've honestly thought we were BFFs, the way he responded to me and not to his actual friend who had just told him she wasn't going; period and shaded him in the process. It was at this moment that I learned:

1. It would serve you best being okay with upsetting people when making decisions that make you genuinely happy and fulfilled.

2. You must understand that people will associate you with being one way, based on their personal feelings. It has nothing to do with you.

3. Be aware of the behavior of those who enjoy posing as victims. They will always find something to be upset with or offended by someone.

4. It's okay to say no!

5. In a time of need, people will need you to express yourself in a way in which they can understand.

A stupid man's report of what a clever man says can never be accurate, because he unconsciously translates what he hears into something he can understand.

— Bertrand Russell

My problem wasn't that I couldn't speak up. It was that I repeatedly chose not to when I knew I needed to. Again, I felt the need to play this "be there for" role for someone merely because this person invited me. Have you ever found yourself playing a role to make someone happy, telling them what needed to hear, although you didn't agree or could care less?

However, at times, the way you communicate has nothing to do with what you say, but more with what the person on the receiving end needs to hear or tries to comprehend. When I told the associate, "I don't really want to go, but since because you invited me, I will go," that statement wasn't what he wanted to hear. He didn't understand. It went against whom he thought himself to be, which then caused him to act as if someone was against him or did him wrong, and when I didn't respond in a way he needed—drama. As I became more aware of these incidents, the foundation for my new earth was laid, and the way of the world had become a little clearer.

Athlete's Tip: Understand that your voice matters, and although I refer to your physical voice, I am more so speaking of your inner voice. When you feel you are being mistreated, taken advantage of, or hurt, speak up! We must stop neglecting ourselves and how we feel when we are in the company of our lovers, best friends, and our families. If you don't want to do something, say you don't. If you don't want to hear about someone's depression, you can say, "Not today." I have not always valued my voice, but that changed. I now have a book because of it.

Chapter 2
DO FOR YOURSELF, ALWAYS.

As 2016 came around, I completely made my way out of my comfort zone and more into who I wanted to be. Meaning, I moved further away from those I loved, I stopped showing up for others' dysfunctions, and I learned how much harmony and joy I could offer myself by simply making a choice and acting upon it. As I began to free myself of spaces where my energy did not genuinely care to be, I started to feel a sense of what enlightened individuals call *light*. During this time, I was spending a large amount of my time alone. Alone with my thoughts, alone in my depression and dysfunction, and I began unlocking the mental clutter that was my childhood. I witnessed a new *woke*—I am not talking Black Power Woke. I mean, *the way of the world* woke. I began feeling less like a victim to my life situations and realized that I've been chosen.

Through my struggles, I am a witness that no one will do for you what you will do for you. More important, it's no one's job to. No one will—nor can they—give you the keys to your success. It's your success! You must either go search for it, on you own, or create it yourself. There is no rulebook to this thing called life—*you gotta do what you gotta do.* But always expect consequences for your actions.

$2,700

Back in 2009, I'd gotten into my first-ever car accident. Luckily, I wasn't severely injured. I could walk and talk after the dust had settled, a little thrown off from being in a state of shock, but overall, I was okay. From this accident, I walked away with a check totaling almost $5,000, and at the time I was only seventeen. A seventeen-year-old with 5K? I was rich! Living in that five-bedroom home—you know, the one my mother allowed the other family to move in—I'd managed to snag a room.

The year prior, my mom completely stopped providing for me, and although we all lived under the same roof, I was paying my mom rent—I'd been paying rent for a long time. Furthermore, at sixteen I developed a slick game of back talk, and I told my mom about herself and how shitty our living situation was, how lazy she was, and so on. We were poor and struggling bad, and the way my mom ran our household just made me furious, so I had to say something. We were one late payment away from being put out on the street, again—which did happen in the months ahead; I grew tired of this.

Aside from talking back and letting my mother know just how I felt, the truth was my mom couldn't afford to take care of me. Prior to getting this check, I'd been working at McDonald's out in BWI Airport, trying to save up to get myself a few essentials—a bed being one of them. We'd been living in this house for about three to four months, and I was crashing on the floor in my room. So, this check couldn't have come at a better time.

With this paycheck, I ran to the furniture store. It was the very first thing I did, and I dropped $2,700 on a brand-

DO FOR YOURSELF, ALWAYS.

new bedroom set. I splurged on a few other things, as you can imagine, but my bed was number one **#SleepSecured**.

Now, because I had to provide for myself, I did not bother to share this check with anyone in my household. I knew the $5,000 would eventually run out, so I needed to hold onto the rest of it for as long as I could. Soon enough, I knew my mother would get upset because I wasn't sharing, and she did, but I had to do what I had to do.

My mom then told my father who stopped by to talk with me. We sat talking for about three hours, and during that time he let know just how much he disapproved of my self-centered ways; he didn't like it. Back then, I spoke with a lot of "Me's" and "I's." In other words, I made things about myself, but I had my reasons. My father said, "You have to stop with all this I-I-I, me-me-me shit." I didn't know how to take this. Because you see, no one was making anything about me. No one cared about how unhappy or uncomfortable I was. No one cared about my well-being overall. So, I took it upon myself to care for myself. I centered my life around myself because I didn't have a choice.

Before my settlement check, no one thought to ask or say, "Hey, Antoine, I know you have a little job, but let me go half with you so you can have something to sleep on at night." My father wasn't called or shown up then. Only I, myself, was going to drop that much money so that I could sleep comfortably as I deserved. From this moment on, I learned I must always do for me—no matter who approves or who doesn't.

After a few months had gone by, my dad thought more about what I had done and what he'd said. He ended up apologizing to me and taking his words back. My dad let me know that I was right to do what I did because had I not done it, I would've still been sleeping on that floor, and it was the truth.

47

In the black community, it's a huge no to speak up to our parents. It's deemed disrespectful, and many of our families cannot even begin to have open and honest conversations—the way the Johnsons do on *Black-ish*—about what's going on in our homes. We can't have family meetings to find out how we can start working together to improve our home environment, our communication with and to one another, or how we, as a family, can merely support each other. We develop this one-for-self mentality. This behavior then spills over into our community—as a whole. If we, as black people, cannot or do not support the men and women in our homes, how can we begin to see the value in supporting and investing in the startup of black businesses? The black men and women who aren't related to us? *Everything connects.*

    I couldn't begin to discuss how I felt living in the projects or being poor because that meant my parents would have had to admit to themselves that they weren't doing the best they could do. Or maybe they were, and they saw nothing wrong with it? After I let my mother know just how I felt about her parenting skills. As a result, she stopped taking care of me. Punish a man for his honesty, and he'll stop telling the truth. I'd then realize that the best thing you could ever do in life is to save yourself first. This situation also helped me realized just why I struggle so much with speaking up.

> **Side Note: In the second chapter of The Four Agreements, Don Miguel speaks about being impeccable with our word. He writes about how a woman comes home after a long and emotional**

DO FOR YOURSELF, ALWAYS.

day of work, feeling exhausted, and with a headache. Meanwhile, in the other room, her daughter is feeling joyful and happy, singing at the top of her lungs. Without thinking, the mother yells out, "Shut up; you have an ugly voice. Can you shut up?" and immediately the little girl is put under a spell. She grows up believing her voice is ugly and that if she talks, she'll continuously annoy others. She'll no longer sing and go off struggling to make friends all because her mom, the woman who loved her unconditionally, said her voice was ugly.

In complete agreeance that girl was me. As a child, and partly as an adult, I lied a lot, only because punishment soon followed when speaking my truth. My family, my household, did not value honesty or cannot stand to hear your reality—the same goes with my employers. In my poor home, to speak my truth or to speak on how I felt would be looked at as ungrateful, and as you read prior, it will have you taking care of yourself.

My childhood was anything but easy—far from it, but it's been these tough times that have shaped me and helped me become aware of so much. It's easy to feel sorry for people like me, who grew up under the conditions that I have, and it's effortless for people like me to feel sorry for themselves. However, *I choose* not to live this way; instead, I humble myself and silently thank the Universe for all that it's shown and given me. I feel I am ten times more likely to succeed simply because of where I come from and because I've been able to hustle my way out. Further,

I refuse to allow life to make me feel as if I am a victim because I am not, despite my life experience. Those of you who are reading this, know that you do have the power to change what you want. You have the ability to make it out of whatever crises you are or will face. Realizing this is **#GOALS!**

I was young and unaware that life situations weren't personal, but when you don't know better—you don't know. I couldn't recognize how my life situation was working in my favor, instead of working against me. You can always measure your destiny by how much BS you go through. As Christians say, "God gives all his hardest battles to his toughest soldiers." yet, while I do not believe in God, I do side with the fact that those who suffer the most are those of us who're supposed to flourish overall, but thrive at what? That's what you must find out.

I believe those who suffer the most are those who have more inspiration to pull from. Those who know great loss or pain are the ones who are supposed to win; all that's needed is figuring out where you need to be, and what you need to do to *win*—this is what it means to build A New Earth. You don't go through what feels like hell to say you've been there, or you've done that, or to stay in the same spot that you were during the tragedy. Through your suffering, a lesson has been given: learn it, grow from it, and apply it as you continue to move on through this world.

Destiny, No Child

Fitness happens to be my calling—not my overall calling, but part of it. I believe everyone's calling, some in more ways than one, is to help. However, for me, because of the challenges that have manifested in my life, I'm able to stay consistent in whatever I want to do in life. In other words, it's where I come from that drives me to wake up every

DO FOR YOURSELF, ALWAYS.

morning at the crack of dawn and push through, even when I don't feel like it. It's where I come from that inspires me to be here for *the people* instead of the systems. It's where I come from that drives me, that motivates me, that keeps me on! It's the hotdog-and-beans-noodles flow, the syrup-sandwiches hustle, and the Kool-Aid ambition that plays a part in my diabetic hunger for what I want and why I will not quit until I get it. It's where I come from that helped me write this eight-chapter book that I did not know I had in me.

I feel I have nothing to lose, so why would I not try? If what I want doesn't work out the way I plan, why wouldn't I try again and take a different approach? Your struggles, the ones that bring you to your knees, the ones that feel like hell on earth, all happened to you for a reason. You owe it to yourself to find out what that reason is. You don't just live after a great defeat—you become.

Before realizing that fitness was part of my calling, I had to find out just what exactly it was about fitness. Should am I supposed to be a personal trainer? Should I start a website? Should I give out advice, freely? Should I build a lifestyle brand and one day a gym facility to give the Everyday Athletes an Everyday space to construct themselves? Should I write a book about my life experiences and share with others just how I began living happier and healthier? Yes, yes, and yes. It's through fitness, which is through my story that I help – giving hope. If I can do this, bro, anybody can do this.

> **Side Note: WardBody started as an idea for underwear because I was tired of my underwear rising as I worked out. Now I'm a rising star! If you sit long enough with your ideas, they'll tell you how to make them happen.**

Athlete's Tip: No one is going to do for you what you must do for yourself. Your life and your well-being should-be centered around you, and it is okay to be selfish. The goal, however, is to lose your ego. Being self-centered or selfish should not make you evil, rude, or nasty; that's ego. Being all about you will, at times, stem from a negative place, a place where you feel no one cares about or honors you, this is an okay place to gain self-centeredness, but do not lead with that attitude. Being selfish is having inner joy, it's *I am joyful, and as long as I have me, I will forever have enough.* Keep in mind that people are just people, and we cannot begin to save one another when we don't have the tools to do so.

The solution, I realized, for me to start living happier and healthier, the way I wanted, was to begin taking control—control of whom I allowed in my space, my surroundings, and my emotions; this is what I hated the most growing up. I felt I had no say in what happened to me: the things I ate, where I slept, what I looked like, or struggles I faced. My caregivers oversaw all these things, and I could not stand it. I couldn't wait until I turned twenty-one to be independent and free. Now, being in my late twenties, I know—without a doubt—it is a must that I am my own person. Therefore, when the time came to celebrate my twenty-sixth birthday, I knew just how to celebrate.

Reaching a level of maturity, where I felt in control of who I was, I felt I needed to celebrate myself. So, for my twenty-sixth birthday, I decided to travel to Los Cabo, Mexico, alone. I wanted to celebrate the fact that my decisions and ideas had driven me out of the ghetto, out of toxic friendships, and helped me align with the life that is me. I was honored to celebrate my independence and my will to take full responsibility for myself, and it felt amazing. Sometimes I forget about everything that I've been through, and I forget to be proud of myself. My life could've taken a turn for the worst. I could've completely given up, but I didn't, and I never knew that this was an accomplishment within itself.

On my actual birthday, I sat in front of a mirror in my suite and cried, telling myself just how sorry I was and how proud I felt. I let myself know just how beautiful I am and how dedicated and inspiring I am—to myself. I celebrated the fact that I taught myself everything I know and was able to stay sane throughout it all.

Overall, taking this trip to Cabo confirmed that no one has my happiness and that I am never without it if I have me. I am enough, and there will never be a shortage of me if I need me. There is nothing I cannot do or get through if I'm one with my *source*.

You Don't Have to Wait!

I believe, when you deny yourself things that you can personally offer yourself, you're held in a space that is not of value, not until a third party sees it or tells you, you are. Speaking from experience, when you don't value yourself, your life, or your time, you begin to produce universal energy that—metaphorically speaking—screams, take advantage of me! By not valuing yourself, you start to invite energy; i.e., people and circumstances into your space that proves that which you feel, and many of these people and things will succeed because you've allowed them.

This then translates into everything else that you do in life. You don't believe you are worthy until someone sees it in you and tells you, you are. You don't feel you are great until permission is given to you to feel this way about yourself, and others acknowledge your greatness. No! *"I am great because I said I am great whether you see it or not! I am worthy because I said I am worthy!"*

Lead with who you are—not with your illusion (ego) of self—and let the rest follow. Your mother and father may have laid your foundation, but they will not, and they cannot give you, you.

> Do not wait: the time will never be 'just right.' Start where you stand, and work with whatever tools you may have at your command and better tools will be found as you go along.
>
> *— Napoleon Hill*

With my newfound independence and control over myself—utterly different from self-control—I began to understand that there will never come a perfect time to offer yourself more of what you need, and you should not wait for others to give you what you feel you deserve. I began embracing new habits, I started writing this book, and I changed my mind about many things, and realized what I wanted, I already had.

Side Note: You need love? Offer it to yourself. Want support? Stand in the mirror and voice to yourself, "I support you!" Your life is complete because you complete it. Nothing about you should stem from the outside world. I vowed to make sure I felt as if I was enough for me. I learned that the Universe has a different method of teaching me things, and at times these teachings came in the form of other people. I used to say that "I needed no one," and I was lying. The truth is I am partly who I am today because of those who either are or were a part of my life. So, in hindsight, I needed everyone who came in and out of my life to bring me their dysfunctions, their dishonesties. I needed people to go against me—or who I thought was me—for me to realize just who I was *not!*

Permission Is Not Needed!

Growing up there weren't conversations going on in my household about chasing dreams or finding what my siblings and I wanted to do with our lives. Education, creativity, and everything else in between weren't a thing. Yes, we all went to school, but by choice. We weren't forced to go to school like some of our peers. It was never instilled in me to participate in anything more significant in life. Not joining the local basketball team, or dance class, not even arts and craft, and I honestly think it had something to do with the fact that I was gay. I believe this made my mother uncomfortable. Being as though, my mother enrolled my sister into our elementary school's Dancing Dolls program, where she danced as a ballerina at school functions, then later in helped my sister enroll into a marching band. My mom also enrolled my little brother into, both our neighborhood football, and basketball team, but I guess this was partly my fault.

   As a child, I never took an interest in anything outside of toys, movies, and cartoons. All I ever excelled at was imagining stuff, and that's not something you need to train for or practice. There's no Little League program for kids who have bright imaginations. You don't win awards and trophies or get scholarships just because you can imagine stuff. However, overall, I did not feel unique growing up, and I never felt as if I had a real talent.

#WARDBODY

For years, I felt that someone had to tell me how special or how smart I was before I could see it in myself. Being told I could do something had been the reason I moved out of Baltimore. It's as if I needed to hear my best friend tell me, *"Antoine, you can leave if you want,"* because once she said it, I left. I was subconsciously seeking permission from others to tell me what I should be, could be, or was allowed to do next.

Later in life, I learned my imagination served me well, and that it was a tool in disguise that few possess. I learned that I'd been leading the pack the entire time. You see, having an imagination means you haven't, subconsciously, put a cap on life—any, and everything is possible and there's no right or wrong, there's no such thing as rules, and most importantly as a black gay man, there's nothing I cannot do, or become. I didn't know this until I started creating WardBody.

However, as a child, no one could recognize my level of intelligence or measure my will to succeed because they identified "being smart" with someone who did well in school and school only – someone who brought home great report cards and knew how to take tests. Whereas my intelligence steamed from the things, I thought about, what I could create, build, or construct. My family couldn't see greatness in me because I didn't identify with a group of people that they deemed talented or great.

However, when I realized my imagination served me well, I realized why I am interested in everything I am. For example, everything I do or enjoy is all about construction, construction of the body, construction of one's life: self-construction. That is, in fact, the definition of WardBody. WardBody means "to construct."

I realized I love constructing/building things from beginning to end, and though it's not a physical talent like

DO FOR YOURSELF, ALWAYS.

basketball or dancing, it does require you to think, plan, and practice. After learning this, I understood why I am into fitness, why I enjoy architecture and interior design and even dating. I now know that I am someone who loves the process of building things and my imagination serves an excellent purpose for all of this.

I know now that you shouldn't wait for someone to see something in you. Nine times out of ten, those same individuals probably cannot recognize greatness within themselves, so how can they begin to see it in you? Even more, why give someone the opportunity to tell you whether, or not, you are great?

Don't wait for someone to see your beauty, your greatness, or your magic. If you feel beautiful, be beautiful; you don't need permission. What you do is not for the likes of others; however, be kind and gracious and do you. As the adult and creator that I am now, I am not waiting for anything or anyone. If I can get started on what I want to see or be a part of, I am going to do it.

> **Side Note: As a creator, asking your consumers what they think about something you want to create is a huge no-no. As consumers, we don't know what we want. As a creator, if you believe in what you are doing, do it with quality. Then give it to us and seek feedback after.**

There will never be a perfect time than right now for you to love yourself, to launch a project, or to embrace new habits. A lot of us procrastinate and make excuses about why we can't do something. We tell ourselves that we need other things to happen before we get started, versus merely starting. Waiting for others will have you sleeping on the floor for three to four months. Trust me: I know this. I lived it.

Athlete's Tip: Before searching for anything—for example, love, support—take some time to define what these things look like to you. In other words, how do you love yourself? Define love and support and base this definition on how you love and cherish yourself. Show yourself what help looks like, what does it mean for someone to be there for you? How are you there for yourself? No one can offer you what you want when you haven't contributed or defined what it is that you want. Most important, no can provide you with anything if you don't give that which you seek to yourself first. Everything you want to experience must first start with you. A team is great, but that's not Success. Chase your goals, live in your love, and find yourself first!

> Don't wait until everything is just right. It will never be perfect. There will always be challenges, obstacles and less than perfect conditions. So, what, get started now. With each step you take, you will grow stronger, more skilled, more self-confident and more successful.
>
> – *Mark Victor Hansen*

The Answer Is No—or Is It?

As time progressed, I revisited a book that I'd once read back when I first moved to New York. Fabulosity: What It Is & How to Get It, written by Kimora Lee Simmons, my idol talks about how the front door is not always open to some of us and that we need to stress other options to get inside wherever we want to be. Kimora then goes on to say that hearing no isn't something that should stop

DO FOR YOURSELF, ALWAYS.

you from pursuing what you believe is for you. Personally, when it comes to goals, no is the Universe telling you to, "Figure out another way." and it was through fitness that I'd learned this.

Just like life, in fitness, there is this thing called variations. A variation is a change or difference in condition, amount, or level, typically with certain limits. For example, when I hit the gym and let's say its chest day, I perform different variations to get the results I want. When lifting weights, as you can imagine, your body gets tired, and your muscles start to resist some of the movements you do. Lifting seventy-pound barbells seven times, six times each is not easy, but like life, you push through, and with perfect formation. However, dumbbell press is just one in many ways you will get the results you want. The plus side of lifting these dumbbells is that if your arms do get tired, and you start to feel as if you cannot do more, but don't want to give up entirely, you have the luxury of adjusting the weight.

Now, the moral of all this is, with my body posing as the opportunity I want in life, if I can figure out different variations to obtain what I want, no is not an option. I can lighten my load and make things easier, yet, while I know taking it easy will not bring me significant results; however, it will bring me a little closer to my goal. I can rest up, come back harder than ever, and **#GETSHITDONE**.

However, I used to take the word no very personal. Meaning, I used to think *no* meant it was over., finished, done, complete. When I first moved to New York, just like many others, I thought I had what it took to model. I got into my head, for some reason, that the only way I would succeed in life was through modeling. I allowed people to excite me and make me believe I had what it took tell me how cute I was, which then convinced me that I had it what it took. I could snag a couple of posters and billboards in Times Square. I could be the face of God knows what.

I put together what I thought was a dope portfolio, and I look back at some of those photos and ask myself, "Why didn't anyone love me enough to tell me to stop?" The pictures were horrible, and I am sure I looked like a complete fool. Further, I put this book together and shopped it to almost every modeling agency in New York. "No," "No," "No," and "Have a great day" was all I heard. I used to laugh at myself because of how nonchalantly people at the front desk would turn me down and send me on my way. I was the joke, and I most certainly got it. However, deep down, a part of me always knew that modeling was not for me. I'm mean. Look at me. I am just too beautiful for that industry. During this time in life, I didn't know what I was working with; I was figuring that part out. So, to hear "No" or "Have a nice day" did something to my self-esteem. For the longest, I wouldn't go as hard in the gym and lift weights because I was so afraid, I would get too big and my chances of being a model would be over. I told myself one day that someone would see something in me, and I would at least walk in BET's *Rip the Runway*. At least, *Rip the Runway*. No?

Months later, I washed my hands with trying to model. My friends would say I gave up too fast and I didn't pursue it hard enough, but I knew it wasn't going to work out because it wasn't organic. I felt nothing like myself when I walked into casting calls with my jaw clenched, trying to be sexy and serious. It was uncomfortable. So, I bowed out and began living my truth, and my purpose found me. Over time I understood, I wasn't supposed to be the face of global brands. I was meant to be the face of my global brand—just like my idol Kimora had been for hers.

DO FOR YOURSELF, ALWAYS.

Athlete's Tip: If you believe you have what it takes to be that someone you want to be, whether it's a model, a singer, or an actress, you owe it to yourself to go all out for it. If you are like me, and you do not feel—100 percent—in what you are doing, or trying to do, is for you, let it go. However, for those who know they are supposed to be doing a specific something, enjoy the challenges you must go through to get to where you want to be. Know that nothing and no one can tell you no if you want what you say you want. You will find ladders, you will jump through windows, or you will dig tunnels. You will do whatever is needed to get into the space that you want to occupy. Also, do not allow others to force you into a box where you genuinely know you don't want to be. Lead with an open mind, and try everything, yet also know when something is not for you.

Journal Entry

July 2, 2010
8:49 pm

Dear Father God,

This is just so crazy, like what is going on. I'm just so lost, dear Father God. We need some major help, dear Father God. Major. What am I to do with these conflicts? Is this the end for my family? Did my mother really give up? Is she serious about her life? I'm mad, angry, sad, upset, shocked, all at the same time. This is just too much. Every time I feel like I'm trying to get somewhere with myself, it's just like something else comes up and hits me. I just pray to you that you help my mother; she needs the most prayer out of everyone, and I just need you to hear me please, dear Father God. I don't/can't forget them and go off and do my own thing because I don't want to feel selfish or low. I'm just very, very upset, dear Father God. I don't want any of my sisters or brother to end up like my mother. I just don't want to see my only brother going down a harsh road, dear Father God, PLEASE HELP ME AND MY FAMILY, PLEASE....

January 1, 2017
8:51 pm

Amazing—that's how I am feeling!! Feeling so ready to take in this new year.

I brought my new year in, in a club on 36th street with my friend Whitney. It was really fun. Lived it up and went straight home.

This year I am planning man. I would like to be more focused, more careful, more aware, more alert, more pulled together, more BUSINESS MINDED!

While accepting like to happen, I am ready to spend $10,000 on WardBody and save as much as I can.

Within the weeks to come, I am ready to sit down with someone and draw out what WardBody will look like.

I am looking to sustain more meaningful friendships. I am happy, bruh. And ready to quit my job!!!

Part Two
LEAD WITH WHO YOU ARE AND LET THE REST FOLLOW

Chapter 3
IT WILL ALWAYS START WITH YOU!

The first few steps you take on any new journey won't get you where you ultimately want to be, but without those first steps, you will always be standing right where you are. When you look toward the future and wonder what it would be like to see your world, your existence, in a way you dreamed, one of the most significant lessons you'll learn is about making the first move. The Universe tends to reward those who are willing to be involved in it and who often take risks.

Once realizing I didn't need permission to create or to build what I wanted to be a part of— or do anything for that matter—all I ever had to do was begin! Life opened-up to me. The way I saw myself living, the healthy lifestyle decisions, whom I want to be, I just had to define what these things look like to me and start doing them. Changing my habits, rewiring myself, and making up my mind that *this is it*; all I had to do was make an effort. However, before realizing I didn't need permission, I thought I had to be at a certain point in my life, in a particular financial position, with a certain reputation and popularity to do or be whom I wanted—to create what I wanted. As I stated in the introduction, I felt I needed to be something or someone other than myself to write my story, instead of simply writing.

As beings, entrepreneurs, or Everyday Athletes, everything we want starts entirely with us. We spend time seeking validation from others and neglect looking to ourselves first. I honestly believe this is the reason why so many men and women turn to the streets, putting themselves at risk and experience needless suffering, addiction, abuse, or contracting HIV or AIDS—especially men, women, and children of the LGBTQ community.

Growing up without a support system or a loving household can play a significant role in your life outcome, causing you to search outside of yourself for things like love, or the need to feel wanted, or a sense of belonging. Which then results in multiple failed attempts at building relationships, or maybe high sexual activity simply because you mistook the basic human need of being touched (non-sexually) with sexual intercourse, that you'll soon grow to regret. However, the goal here is to become aware. What do I lack? As a child, what was I denied? How have the things that I've been denied play a role in my adult life? How are they causing me to feel, to act, or to believe about myself? A simple piece of awareness can help stop the ongoing cycle that is you. Do not be afraid of you, to unpack the mental clutter that has been you. Do not try to forget, or run away from, or try desperately to hide (yourself) from yourself. You must acknowledge, and you must accept. It's the only way.

Know that you are never without love if you have you.

IT WILL ALWAYS START WITH YOU!

I am aware that we all grow up differently and that some of our struggles may be more brutal than others. However, please know that all you seek is already in you.

How does the Everyday Athlete take the first step on their journey to living a happier and healthier lifestyle?

We Become Self-Aware.
Becoming self-aware, we eliminate the opportunity to self-victimize / self-sabotaging behavior. By making a conscious decision to be self-aware, Everyday Athletes develop a keen eye for what we allow or disallow to take place in our existence. We understand, by allowing ourselves to be who we genuinely are, we then manifest genuine energy, people, and circumstances.

We Make an Effort.
Whether it's eating right or applying a new theory to our life situation, Everyday Athletes make an effort to be who they want to be and create what they want to see. We pride ourselves in putting in time to get to know who we are, inside and out—to listen to ourselves. To exercise what we believe in or stand for.

We Become What We Want to Attract.
(But Do Not Fake It until We Make It)
Ask, and It Is Given. Everyday Athletes understand, once we begin taking steps to get what we desire or become whom we wish to become, we will then attract like-minded people into our lives. The Law of Magnetism says, "Who you

are is whom you attract." If you want to be around evolving people, become an evolving person. Simply be; do not try.

We Hold Ourselves Accountable.
Whether it with our Finances, health, careers, or relationships, we hold ourselves personally accountable and take action to improve any area of our lives where we want to see progress. Everyday Athletes understand that no one will give us what we desire and that we must always push forward in our time of need.

We Stay Committed.
No matter how long it takes, how hard it gets, or who can't see the full vision, Everyday Athletes remain committed. Our belief in ourselves runs deep, and we believe that the payoff for our success will make the time sacrificed worthwhile; actually, we know the payoff will make the time sacrificed worthwhile.

> *Athlete's Tip:* To move forward, you must hold yourself at a level of commitment and dedication, with high integrity—especially when no one is looking because that's when you are who you really are. Don't just say you're committed; prove it to yourself. Whatever or wherever Everyday Athletes dream of being, they know they will not get there unless they put one foot in front of the other and simply **#GETSHITDONE**.

Question Everything!
What is God? Who is Santa Claus? Why do you go Easter egg hunting for Easter eggs when rabbits don't lay eggs? How did a rabbit become the mascot for Easter? Why are white people uncomfortable when a black person says,

nigga? Is Sambo the name of the first black Buddha in East Asia? Does every racial slur toward black people come from something positive that turned into something negative during slavery? Is voodoo real, and is it considered "bad" because black people lived by it? Why wasn't it taught that Christopher Columbus never reached North America? Did Tom ever catch Jerry? Why is it that if a black cat crosses your path, it's deemed bad luck? Are all other cats' good luck? What is luck? Why is the workday eight hours a day, five days a week? Why do we fight so hard to hold on to traditions? Are we really the chosen ones? Why is Thurgood Marshall praised more than Nate Turner? If Jesus died for our sins, why is it said that we shouldn't sin? Did he die for nothing? Why do you think you are worthy to be in a relationship, and witness real love, when you haven't start loving yourself?

"The important thing is not to stop questioning," part of a longer quote that ends with "Never lose a holy curiosity." Albert Einstein thought that questioning and curiosity were the keys to learning. He was very aware of this problem many years ago, when he said, "It is a miracle that curiosity survives formal education," followed by, "I never teach my pupils. I only attempt to provide the conditions in which they can learn." In a world of fabrication, intended deceit, unexpected error, and oblivious intellectual mediocrity, it's an alarming task to convince other people of the importance of asking questions, let alone finding absolute truth among the contradictive chaos that is human science and morality. As individuals, we grow to learn and develop habits, facts, traits, and talents, based on information that those who came before us were either taught or told was *the truth*, and with no evidence or facts.

    I am specifically speaking about our grandmothers and grandfathers and the slave mentality that has been handed down from their mothers and fathers, who then passed it down to our mothers and fathers, which made its way down to us and begin called *Tradition*. Slavery was never a choice; this, we all know. However, aside from slavery being a system that was—and still is—created to oppress black and brown people, it, too, is a mindset, which in fact, is a choice. Furthermore, not questioning those who identify themselves as the Authority can stunt your growth and leave you believing what is, shall always be. However, those who feel they shouldn't be questioned are the problem, such as your mother or your father, teachers, your boss, police officers, the government, or white people in general. All these roles thrive off control and ego, some more than others, and to question them goes against whom they believe they are and the role that they play.

> **Side Note: This behavior is why I side with the Joker more than Batman. If God is God, why would he not want you to question him? Allegedly, a man who knows it all, who has seen it all, has done it all and created you in the process, knows you don't know it all. Why would he not expect for you, as a clueless, curious being to question him, or to ask questions, period? This too is programming. Why must I fear a person who made me? Why would you want anyone to fear you? Control! It's in our school systems, our jobs, and our neighborhoods. A true God is a servant to his people.**

IT WILL ALWAYS START WITH YOU!

For me, questioning everything in life has been an essential key to existing. I've come to know that despite the roles that many identify with, people lie; they don't have much experience—if any. They abuse their power and position, and sometimes people just flat out don't know much with what they speak. Questioning everything is the key to a happier and healthier life.

I understand that no one is going to give me the education or knowledge that I desire, so I must go search for it. I read an African proverb that said, "Beware of the naked man who offers you clothes," which means beware of people who have never been married but give advice, freely, on how to have a happy marriage. The same goes for a person who is overweight supplying dieting tips, environmentalists who do not recycle, and politicians who send their children to private schools while making speeches on the virtues of public schools.

Coming from a black household, we, unlike our white counterparts, do not have the luxury of questioning—or cursing out—our parents. Which then hinders our curiosity and leads to the breaking of so many house rules, which then results in many of us being kicked out and homeless. Because our parents think, "Because I said so," is the answer to everything. Black moms and dads around the world do not believe in giving their children explanations. They make it very clear who's "the boss." Questioning authority figures can get you either punished or, in other countries, killed. Further, true leaders don't label themselves as "authority." They don't need to.

#WARDBODY

Not having the option of trying to figure out why something is the way it is can cause you to relive or go through the same things, repeatedly. Sometimes you need to question yourself and ask, "Self, why am I making this same mistake again, or is it even a mistake at this point? What do I want in life?" Am I sure I want to go through with this Marriage?" I learned that not having the privilege to confidently ask when, where, what, how, who, and why played a significant role in what I accepted in all areas of my life: jobs, friends, and love.

For example, not knowing my worth has made the process of negotiating my salary at work foreign or nonexistent, in most cases. Where I'm from, getting a job offer meant there was nothing to think about or to consider—you should be satisfied that someone is offering you a position within their company making $8.75 an hour, even if the standard pay rate for that position is $13 an hour.

> **Side Note: My first job in New York City paid only $8.75 an hour. I worked as a part-time front desk attendant at a Muay Thai Gym in Soho, where gym memberships ranged from $300 to $1,000+ for private lessons. I'd research the average wages for a part-time front desk attendant in New York and found salaries ranged from $13 to $15 an hour, yet, said nothing—I don't know how I made it through 2014.**

If I interviewed for a position, and the average salary ranged from $50K to $75K, and I had more than enough experience, yet was only offered $45K, I would not speak up and ask, "But the market in New York for this role typically pays (XYZ), and I have more than enough experience. Why am I getting this lowball offer?" Because of my humble beginnings, I didn't find it "normal" to question an employer who was interested in having me be a part of his or her team. If someone offers me $45K, I guess I'll have to accept that I am only worth $45K. No!

When we question the things around us and why they are, we allow ourselves a much more vivid image of the reality of our lives. In understanding the truth in comparison to the apparent facts that most of us actively participate in without question, I promise that you will get a better grasp of how the world really works and how you play into it all. Questioning is a step in the right direction to living happier and healthier. You have the right to question anything you feel the need to, and you should.

I have one more question!

> *Athlete's Tip:* Forever listen with an intent to understand, but research what's being taught or told on your own time. Don't allow someone else to tell you; find out for yourself. You'll never know what you can handle, what you are capable of, or what you interpret differently by continually listening to others. Find out on your own! We are not here to persuade people to live how we see fit or to act how we want them to. However, what's important is to have your own perspective. No matter how right our mothers and teachers believe they are, it's important to question their opinions and theories of what they deem to be the truth. We must continuously question those who influence our conclusions.

Undo Your Childhood

The undoing of my childhood came about when I realized I no longer want to create excuses for myself. I surrendered–

and by *surrendered*, I mean *accepted*—to the process of undoing. I was tired of being depressed and wondering, "Why me?" I began being very real with myself, asking myself, "Why not me? Who am I? Do I think just because I went through some little problems in life that someone owes me something? Do I think life is simply supposed to favor me and cut me a break because poor Antoine is sad? Do I think because I said I wanted to be great, greatness is just supposed to find me?" I am a tough-love kind of guy, as you can see, and these are the kind of pep talks I give myself.

By undoing, for starters, I've learned how much I enjoy dating men who appeal to my inner child, meaning I enjoy dating experiences that are filled with fun and excitement and adventure. A man who inspires me to jump out of airplanes, ride roller coasters, swim with sharks, all while caring for me genuinely. Sharing moments of fun, and excitement knowing that there's more to life than how we look or what we wear, or what we mean to others because as a child a lot of this stuff I've never had. Things like learning how to snowboard, hitting up Dave and Busters to play and lose every game—which took me until I was twenty-six to experience, yet, now as an adult I am aware that any dating experience that is brimming with adventure, honesty, fun, and light is something I thoroughly enjoy and want to be a part of forever.

Once I realized that undoing what was, in fact, an actual thing, I began spending a ton of time alone and got to know myself. I started accepting everything that has been, and I stopped resisting what was. I gave everything the opportunity to flow through me, instead of holding onto it as if it were my actual identity: where I came from, how I grew up, and the mental and physical damage that took place during my childhood.

Yes, I come from Oodles of Noodles and Section 8. I come from manipulation and physical and emotional abuse disguised as love, but that was no longer whom I chose to be. In fact, I realized, I never chose anything because I never had options. Options to be who or what I wanted to be, where I lived, where I grew up, or what I ate, but the moment I began undoing, it hit me that I had the opportunity now! I am no longer where I come from, and I've given myself permission to drop those habits and recreate myself.

By merely undoing one part of my childhood, I began to understand just how much of a product I'd been. For example, growing up in a broken, dysfunctional household and trying to experience a relationship before undoing your childhood is dangerous! Personally speaking, I believe we should try to hold off on building with others until we've completed the undoing process or, at least, work to become aware of the trauma that has unfolded in our lives. For many of us, especially black gay youth, how we grew up was not positive, and the pain or hurt caused by our families, we now think *"well this is just me,"* making it someone else duty to help us work on ourselves. We are no one's responsibility but our own.

> **Side Note: We all have battles that we are fighting, but do not use this as an excuse to live or act recklessly. Get a jump start on your relations, friendships, and bonds by working on yourself first! Do not wait until you enter a relationship to want to correct toxic behavior. Make a conscious effort to do so beforehand. No one deserves your brokenness.**

#WARDBODY

    As children we are subconsciously conditioned, programmed instead, to carry others pain, guilt, fear, and sometimes truths. During my undoing process, I realized I had a deep fear that didn't really concern me, but because it happened to so many around me, it somehow made its way into my subconsciousness. I feared that if or whenever I entered a relationship, I'd be cheated on. Silly, right? This programming started, of course, in my home. The year before my mom passed away, my sister and I were having a conversation about men, and our mother overheard us talking and said to me, "Antoine is never going to be able to keep a man because he wants too much." and it's something I live with to this day. From my friends, both female and male, my mother, my sister, I don't know anyone who hadn't experienced infidelity.

    It wasn't until I was able to undo that I'd allowed myself to see things for what they were. I grew to know certain people bring out certain things in us, and a lot of us aren't willing or mature enough to have conversations with ourselves about what we want in relationships, to begin with, meaning we never took time out to define what a healthy relationship looks like, knowing we never witnessed one growing up. So, we enter situations not addressing what we are looking to get out of the experience with others, both romantically and with friends. If I had a nickel for how many times I've heard, "*It just happened.*" in response to "*How did you guys decide to become official?* Also, a lot of us think having a relationship equates with success, and for many, it can. But I promise you this feeling of success will not last. A relationship with another person cannot be your means to an "end" or something that makes you complete, especially if you are in your twenties. You need to want more, out of yourself and your relationships.

    However, after undoing, I noticed my fear of being

cheated on did not reflect my reality, meaning, the reality of my life did not revolve around men, nor had I experienced moments where I could've possibly been cheated one, given I'd never had a boyfriend. I have, however, been in a situation where I felt a relationship was the next step, but it never happened—which am I am so thankful for—but I've never had a horrible history with men. I wasn't in scandals with someone else BF, or physically had to fight someone over another, no one doing me dirty on the gram, or having to find out intel from, the person I was dating, ex-BF. For the most part, I never dreamed of being so attached to someone—well there was that one time—that I make him feel as if I own him, which is what a ton of relationship, in our twenties is: ownership.

As Osho said, "Real love never waits to be rewarded, even to be thanked. If the thankfulness comes from the other side, love is always surprised—it is a pleasant surprise because there was no expectation. You cannot frustrate real love because there is no expectation in the first place. And you cannot fulfill unreal love because it is so rooted in the expectation that whatsoever is done always falls short."

When you don't know you are worthy, though, or you don't see yourself as a privilege, you go against yourself, accepting less than you deserve. However, through undoing my childhood, I've learned that my reality is not others' reality and vice versa. My Mom not realizing her self-worth had nothing to do with my self-esteem, and the same goes for everyone else I knew. I had to understand that we all bring out something different in one another. I might bring out something completely different in a man than what my mom, friends, or sister have, causing him not to feel the need to cheat on me. But more so, if he did, his infidelity has nothing to do with me.

#WARDBODY

Understand that many of your beliefs and thoughts are not yours. At times we're forced to believe—in what we do because of those who came before us. We become Muslims, Jews, or Christians due to someone else's beliefs and traditions, which is unfair, yet, while some parents—like Will and Jada Pinkett Smith, for example—who allow their kids to create themselves and their reality, this isn't the case for many of us. If we analyze ourselves part by part, from our definition of success to our self-worth, we will find solid links to our childhood. For you to experience life as you see fit, question everything, and unlearn the pessimistic lessons and reteach yourself.

My life wouldn't be my life had I not undone my childhood and gotten to know myself. Investing in my health, waking up at 4:00 AM every morning to hit the gym, to read or write, or just walking to my local coffee shop to grab a bagel—all these things wouldn't be a thing. Why? Well for starters, there aren't coffee shops in McCulloh Home Projects or a gym or organic food in markets and the only time you are out running at 4:00 AM is if 5-0 is chasing you or you're trying to get away from being robbed. Living in the ghetto is a lifestyle and a mindset that I had to undo. Growing up in the ghetto, no one teaches you how to live life, you're taught how to survive in life, and while I'm very appreciative of all the lessons I've learned, I am much happier to say I made it out.

Leon F. Seltzer, PhD, author of *The Vision of Melville and Conrad: A Comparative Study* and former English professor at Queens College and Cleveland State University, has listed nine dysfunctional programs you may have subconsciously brought into adulthood. Athletes, please take note:

1. Do you underestimate your potential—or believe that whatever success you've had is not reflective of your capability?
Did either of your parents say or suggest to you that you didn't have what it takes to succeed? That you shouldn't set your sights too high? Or possibly that you weren't as smart, talented, or qualified as your siblings or other family members?

2. Do you consistently find faults with yourself and validate the notion that you're a terrible person or not cut out for something?
Do you beat yourself up—or admit to fault—before anyone else might? Do you focus on your shortcomings? Obsess about how could anyone really like you (if they truly knew you)? Question your motives?

3. Do you regard yourself as undeserving—or believe that you have little to no right to ask for what you want or need?
Is self-assertion difficult for you? Do you deprive yourself of things you would enjoy or that would contribute to your welfare? Do you even reject others' attempts to offer you what you desire because you feel insufficiently worthy to accept their gifts or assistance?

4. Do you see yourself as an outsider or an outcast—and believe that you don't, or can't, fit in with others?

Did you have problems blending in with your peers? Did you feel as if you didn't belong in your family? Were you criticized or made fun of for being different or in some way peculiar? Did any of your physical characteristics seem to set you negatively apart from others? And in your present life, do you sometimes feel like a pariah, as though you're a stranger in a strange land?

5. Do you perceive yourself or perhaps the whole world as untrustworthy—and believe that you should be suspicious of yourself or those around you?

Did your parents distrust you? Were you tempted to behave in untrustworthy ways, for that was the only way you could get your basic needs met? Did your parents teach you not to trust anyone because they had become disillusioned with others, or they projected their own deceitfulness or duplicity onto other people? In which ways—direct or indirect—might your parents have prompted you to see yourself as inherently dishonest?

6. Do you devalue or belittle yourself, making yourself believe that you're less worthwhile than others, and do you often sell yourself short?

Did your caretakers typically disregard your needs or make light of them and send a message that your needs didn't matter? Did you buy into their attitude when they discounted the legitimacy of what was important to you? Among other things, ask yourself whether you've adjusted to this self-minimizing viewpoint by subordinating your needs to others in an effort to earn their love and acceptance (which is how you might have gotten acceptance from your parents).

7. Do you view yourself as codependent, as more responsible for others' welfare than for your own?

Closely related to #6 above, did your parents give you the message that you were selfish—and thereby unacceptable—whenever you prioritized your own needs? Did they hold you responsible for catering to their needs? Maybe someone told you that it was your job to take care of your younger siblings? Were you taught, through their conditional approval, that it was virtuous to sacrifice yourself for others—mainly, your family and people who said they loved you? Or were you made to feel that your proper role was to defer to the wishes of others—and to deny your own?

8. Do you perceive yourself as defenseless or weak—and so live your life as a helpless victim or as excessively dependent on others?

Growing up, were you overprotected, given the message that you were frail or fragile and couldn't fend for yourself? Might your parents have instilled in you their own childhood fears and insecurities? Did you—and do you still—have problems with anxiety? Maybe you see the world as menacing? Do you see yourself as avoidant or risk-adverse?

9. Do you see your feelings as only adding to your vulnerability—so you don't allow yourself to express powerful emotions?
Did either (or both) of your parents criticize or possibly make fun of you when you cried, got angry, or showed fear? Might they have ignored your feelings, making you feel even more alone or isolated when you couldn't help but let them out? Did they shame you for being overcome with emotion—making you feel as if you were "soft" or a "sissy" for having feelings or unacceptable as the girl or the boy they expected you to be?

If you identified with any of the nine dysfunctional situations that are listed above. I would like to offer you a brief, step-by-step Cognitive Behavioral program that I have personally used to help undo what *was*.

BECOME AWARE!
To undo the trauma that has been your childhood, you must first make yourself aware of what was. Yes, that's right—acknowledge it. Allow yourself to feel, experience, or relive all of what has been; this means your belief system and how it grew to be what it is. "Men aren't shit!". What has happened to make you feel this way? "I am unlovable." Who confirmed this?

SAY IT!

Allow yourself to know, both physically and mentally, the details of what has happened to you, or what you would like to undo that you believe is taking your power (i.e., "I have been sexually assaulted by (XYZ)," "I don't feel smart," "I am insecure," "I feel abandoned," "I don't feel beautiful/pretty/handsome."). Perhaps you've felt as I have; no one cared about you as a child, resulting in you not feeling special about yourself, or that there's nothing special about you. "I don't feel special. I don't feel that there's anything special about me." Be honest with yourself.

TELL SOMEONE!

Only when/if you are ready. There's power in being vulnerable: trust me. At your pace, allow a close friend to know your secret, or what you've been dealing with, or how your mom made you feel when you were eleven (even if you are now thirty-two or forty-five). Talk to your favorite aunt. Fill her in with what you've been dealing with as a child. Maybe hire a paid professional to help you with unpacking. It feels good to allow a trusted someone to come into that space you've been running away from and offer you a hug and tell you that it's going to be okay.

PREPARE FOR A CHANGE!

Again, both mentally and physically. Start to prepare for the negative pushback and emotions that will surface from close friends and family when you decided enough is enough, and you began to draw lines and set boundaries. After working through step 3, I hope you'll start to understand that although what has happened—has happened, it doesn't mean it has to continue. You no longer must be who you were; permit yourself. You can keep people dear to your heart and love them from a distance as you move forward in life. Popping pills to help you forget, abusing weed to help you relax, or drinking profusely to help you cope is no longer the answer. From here on out, you deal with everything up front and head on. There's no need to medicate to forget/cope/or dismiss. It's time to remember, confront, accept and boss up!

DO THE WORK!
As I stated before, it will always start with you. Begin doing the physical work. Depending on what you are dealing with—maybe you have unresolved issues with your dad, or perhaps it's your mom. Call them up and ask to talk. Let out everything you've been discussing with your friends or your favorite Aunt. It's time to start doing The Real work. Maybe you are someone like me who suffers from social anxiety. Join a book club, and get your feet wet with meeting like-minded individuals. Whatever it is you are dealing with, begin putting in physical work to conquer it.

BEGIN IMPROVING YOUR SELF-IMAGE!
Who are you now versus who you've been? Start to identify spaces, people, and things that make

you feel good about yourself. Buying yourself flowers, going to the movies, going to the spa, bike riding—whatever it is, do it, and perhaps do it alone; this is the essential part in improving your self-image. Who are you within these moments of happiness and joy? When there's no one else around, and it's just you?

WRITE IT OUT!
Every night or every morning, or both write out how you feel. Keep a record of your days. Journal your positive days, and your not-so-great days. Write out how you are feeling and try to dissect where that feeling is coming from; again, say it out loud. What happened? Who was involved? What role did you play in it?

The goal here is to always come face-to-face with the trauma that lives inside of you or that you may have hidden away from yourself (and occasionally use to help you feel sorry for yourself because life isn't offering you what you want.) It's time to become aware of it, to acknowledge it, and to accept it. Don't continue to ignore your trauma any longer. If you are looking for a sign to deal with a death, a financial loss, an ex, an eviction, a failed attempted at something; this is it! Stop allowing pain and struggle to use you, and instead let's use it. To know better is to do better. Let's start undoing folks.

> *Athlete's Tip:* Dear Athlete, the key to seeing yourself in a genuinely more favorable light is to develop the ability to question everything and undo your childhood. Free yourself from adverse events, and self-sabotaging habits

#WARDBODY

that may have unfolded in your youth. Let's call this an "existential makeover." Remember that if your life hasn't been particularly successful, it doesn't signify that it lacks the potential to be.

Chapter 4
THE POWER OF GOING AT IT ALONE.

After undoing parts of my childhood and healing the child in me, I discovered I was someone who'd suffered from child neglect and borderline abandonment. Growing up, I never felt a part of my family. More so, I never knew who was part of my family, or who my mom just decided to call our "cousins"; you know how we do. Adopted into a few different families, I grew up believing men that my mom was dating, were my Uncles. Just sick! Nevertheless, when I say my family, I mean my immediate family.

Feeling like I didn't fit in with my family, I grew up separated from them—disconnected, somewhat. Throughout my teenage years, before moving away from my mother and siblings, I would lock myself in my room and sit alone for hours, sometimes days at a time. During this time, I was trying to figure out this gay thing. There was no gay figure in my life or anyone who understood gay culture or what it meant to be gay. I had no one to talk to or learn from, and at the time, everyone under my roof judged others who were gay; I was so uncomfortable. So, sitting alone in depression—lost-ness, really—I just wrote out everything I felt and tried to understand myself. Imagine someone in a room posing as the therapist and the patient, that was me.

Although my mom said she was accepting of me being gay, I still would hear things like, "man up," or she'd call me a bitch. I was called Faggies by everyone in my household. So, at times it was very hard trying to accept who I was when where I came from disapproved and made fun of me. My father, however, has never disrespected me in this way. He has never made fun of me or called me out of my name. Which is wild because I was expecting it from him the most.

Further, although my father had accepted me and the fact that I love men, how and where does a heterosexual man (or woman) who has never experienced homosexuality begin discussing what it means to be Homosexual? I felt disconnected from my family because I both mentally and emotionally was. So, instead of trying to become open, I closed myself off from everyone and sat alone, quietly; this was the first time that I honestly felt lonely.

Though, over time being alone and not feeling accepted played a different role in my life, instead of feeling the pressure to be a part of. I became inspired to become my friend. I accepted what I was—a gay man—and got to know this Homosexual being that is myself. What are my likes and my dislikes? Do I understand my emotions and my feelings? Am I a bottom, am I a top, or do I like both? Am I a political gay? A muscle head gay? Am I a church gay? I began dissecting every inch of me, and by the end of it all—which took place over the course of 5 years—I'd fallen completely in love with who and what I was. Now as an adult, my loneliness has become more of solitude, and I choose to live in solitude rather than feel as if I am alone or lonely. Being cast out, or not fitting in with my family, I have been able to find the joy and appreciation in sitting alone in a space that is of peace, both inside and out.

Being able to spend time alone with oneself is an accomplishment. You are who you are when you're by yourself. Embracing aloneness helps you accept all that you are, and it also enables you to grow your confidence, but more importantly, being alone teaches you that validation is not something that lives outside of you.

> **Side Note: If you only do things when you are in the company of others; i.e., drinking, smoking, or even going to the gym, understand that this being you become is not "you", and you should stop doing whatever "it" is all together. Again, you are who you really are when there's no one around. So, if you only do drugs around certain people, you are simply being triggered. The goal is to understand why you feel compelled to do such things when in the presence of those selected individuals, and be honest with yourself.**

Personally, being forced into aloneness helped me realize just how free I am. I don't have to abide by the status quo if I don't want to. I don't need to be known or for you to constantly see me. I don't need to be heard, nor do I need the latest. I don't need to be down with every little thing that takes place in society. I am free to come and go as I please, and I don't need to outsource validation. I am enough, and that's my power.

> *Athlete's Tip:* The Everyday Athlete knows to schedule some quality time alone to help focus on what's essential. Taking time out for ourselves to study, practice, meditate, or unlock

and unleash new ideas is critical to living happier and healthier lives. The Everyday Athlete understands that we can never be alone, not when we have ourselves, yet, If we ever feel as if we are alone, we embrace it because sometimes being alone is an upgrade.

Right after a breakup is the most common time when loneliness creeps in, which in many cases understandable. Our lover was someone we shared massive energy with and invested heavenly in, from shared secrets to building a space where the two of us could coexist in truth. Losing this person can sometimes make you feel lost, or sometimes, it can feel like death. Still, even from this painful experience, we can learn something. We can understand that we suffer for a reason, and it's because we became too attached to whatever left our lives.

We associate loss with failing and fail to realize that relationships need to end for us to grow, and to become whom we are supposed to become. We grow attached to a feeling, idea, or emotion of what used to be, that our ego told us "needs to be," making ourselves feel as if life cannot go on without that ex. Sometimes we make ourselves physically sick.

Detachment is a lesson that I believe everyone should practice. Now, I'm not saying you shouldn't care about people, or you should try not to be in love. What I'm saying is make yourself aware when you begin to project yourself onto the person you are dating. Eckhart Tolle said it best: "If a fish is born in your aquarium and you call him John, write out a birth certificate, tell him about his family history, and two minutes later, he gets eaten by another fish—that's tragic." Love is freedom. The moment you feel love and experience caring for another, you began to project yourself onto that thing or person and make that thing yourself, and that is selfish.

Understand that it all comes, and it all goes, and the goal is to let it. Success means understanding that alone time is when you should either love who you are or get to know more of who you are.

To Fill Voids or to Fill Self

My personal life has always been an area where I am the most sensitive and secretive. I have been known not to tell the full truth when it comes dating, simply because I choose not to. Not everyone needs to know what I am doing or who I am doing it with—not even my family. I have yet to take someone home to meet my parents or to introduce a man or a boy as my boyfriend. I am in no rush to do so. But I will say, as an adult, I do enjoy dating. I enjoy the space that's created over time where both of us can exist and just get to know each other without noise, thoughts, and opinions from any source outside of ourselves. I enjoy establishing a friendship with the person I date and creating a space where both of us can communicate about anything, openly and honestly.

However, like undoing my childhood, before getting to a place where I felt secure within myself, I had to undo my past dating experiences with men. I'd learned in the past that dating wasn't really dating for me. I honestly didn't start dating until I was twenty-four, and from twenty-four to twenty-six, I have dated only two people. The reason I know I have dated only these two individuals is that when dating them, I felt as if I was my complete self. I was utterly self-aware, I remained in a positive space, and I genuinely liked them for them.

I'm aware of this because during a time of me dating, I thought I was experiencing love, yet I couldn't recognize myself. We will talk more about his in a second.

Young adults, especially those of us who come from abandonment, have a strong desire to want others to fill what we believe we're missing in ourselves. I believe many people enjoy feeling as if they matter to others. The people we date or become friends with help us feel this. Then, unconsciously, we set up obstacles to see how much someone cares about us. The moment our lovers or family members do not complete the obstacles that we have subconsciously set out for them, we take it as they don't care, and that no-one-loves-me emotion we felt as kids resurfaces. Simply because our lover never played our game. However, you, as a being, need to know that no man, woman, baby, car, vacation, or any amount of money can fill what's missing inside of you. It's not healthy or fair to put your abandonment issues on someone else.

Your void is your void, and you simply need to work on yourself to fill it. Seeking completeness outside of ourselves is how many people end up in abusive relationships, whether it's emotional, physical, or mental. They start to believe, "This is what I deserve." If you've never taken time out to work on yourself, your sense of feeling like a victim will repeatedly attract abusers. Completeness cannot come from anyone outside of you. Relationships end, babies grow up, money comes and goes, and jobs are lost. Spend some time alone with yourself and work on you.

THE POWER OF GOING AT IT ALONE.

In my early twenties, someone tried to use me to feel a void within himself, and I ended up taking this very personally when I shouldn't have. During my early twenties I was insecure, and I used to measure my self-worth and my attractiveness by whether another man saw me attractive or not. But I quickly learned that everything that glitters is not gold and sometimes the prettiest people are usually the most damaged.

There'd been this guy— let's call him Wade— who had been interested in getting to know me. The way we et was very interesting too. However, he was attractive and had a certain level of popularity in the Baltimore. I don't know why this matter to me, but it did. I was twenty-one, and he was twenty-three/four. The first time Wade and I met, I was not my polished self, meaning I needed a haircut. I later learned he was indeed into appearances and cared much more about how he looked than I did. Now, I take care of myself, but I am not that guy who always looks done up from head to toe. I am okay with who I am, haircut or no haircut.

Furthermore, the next time we met, I had a haircut, and his affection toward me was a little different. As inconsequential as this moment seemed, I locked it in my memory bank and held onto it. Little did I know, it was a piece of a larger puzzle.

As we continued getting to know each other, I learned that Wade was fresh out of a relationship. I forget how long the relationship was, but I know he had been single for maybe three or four months before meeting me. After discussing his past, I learned who Wade's ex-boyfriend was and immediately saw that he had a type. As time went on, I noticed that he compared the two of us a lot, more so our physical stature. Being already insecure, I found it overly uncomfortable. During this time in my life, I had just begun to include weight lifting in my workouts, but I wasn't lifting heavy weights. However, Wade's ex-boyfriend was something straight out of WWE. Meanwhile, I was under construction trying to figure out what my **#FitnessGoals** were., One time, Wade told me, "Lil Bow Wow [not the ex's real name] is much bigger than you. Like, his arms are much bigger than yours, and his hands are a little softer." I held onto this moment for so long because it played a part in how I saw myself at that time. I felt I wasn't good enough, and I attracted that energy into my life.

There was another time Wade watched me as I walked from his car to my apartment and later told me he wanted to see how I walked—to see if I "walked gay". I felt very uncomfortable. There I was, already insecure, and I had someone picking out every flaw about me. But this was my fault, and I'll tell you why in a minute. When the time came for Wade and me to stop getting to know each other, I was a little bummed. I really did like him, or I thought I did, although I knew he had superficial values and a ton of baggage from his previous relationship. Still, I was willing to stick it out and allow him to continue chipping away at my self-esteem.

Wade was clearly disrespecting me. However, I stopped being a victim to his disrespect the moment I became aware of it and continued to allow him to do it. But at twenty-one, you don't know better. You think, this is how things go, and the truth is it isn't. Wade and I both had a void that needed filling. My void was so deep that I was mentally willing to accept what I knew I did not deserve, and I was okay with someone dragging me through the mud and comparing me to his iRobot ex-boyfriend, just to say I had someone.

I took this situation very personally, but after undoing it, I learned that this entire time in my *life* had nothing to do with me, personally. Wade had not fully healed from his previous relationship, and because he was so unaware, he couldn't see how his attempt to recreate what *had been* was now hurting others and himself. More important, he didn't care. He dropped his baggage off on anyone who would be willing to carry it. And as a naive twenty-one-year-old, with no sense of awareness, I felt compelled to do so.

> **Side Note: When moving on to any new relationship or any new dating situation, you need to make sure you aren't carrying baggage like this around with you. You should take just as much time—if not more—you've spent putting into dating someone and heal yourself. Don't be so quick to move on, unloading your emotional distress onto someone else. This also includes sex. Deal with what you must before offering yourself, or your body, to another.**
>
> **Your insecurities are yours, no one else's. It's not fair, nor is it normal, to constantly dive into new relationships with men or women, bringing unresolved issues from the previous relationships or "situationships" that you were in. If you've dated someone and your experience with the person was tragic or unhealthy, even if it wasn't, you should take a year or three off to learn who you now are and to undo whatever was.**

So many people experience hurt and try to cover it up with another being, looking for their savior, their best friend or lover, their one and only. Spend some time alone and be all those things to and for yourself! No one deserves being hurt by you and trying to save you, all at the same time.

#WARDBODY

No one deserves your baggage. You should not try to drag someone else into your pit of hell. It's unfair.

Over the years, Wade and I have kept in contact, communicating with each other to this day. He has apologized and admitted that I didn't really stand a chance of getting to know him because he hadn't fully accepted what had happened between him and his ex. Wade said that he had tried to date me based on his past and what he was used to. He had developed the same attitude and behavior pattern that his ex-boyfriend had toward him and had led with these same patterns when dealing with me. In other words, he became the person who had mistreated him, and he'd treated me the same way. And the cycle continued.

Had I not undone all of this and gotten to know myself, I probably would've been leading with a feeling that I wasn't good enough, or I could've possibly become Wade and Wade's ex and began treating the new men who walked into my life the same way Wade treated me. Worrying about how they walk, how much they lift, or if they lift at all, and so on. Furthermore, the truth was, what Wade had given me had nothing to do with me. Was it unfair and selfish? Absolutely! But I had to learn that what people do to you is never about you.

A lot of us cannot begin to see the lessons that are to be learned in dating someone. For starters, no one should own you, and you should not want to be owned. That is not real love.

> The ordinary love pretends too much. The real love is non-pretentious; it simply is. The ordinary love becomes almost sickening, syrupy, drippy, what you call "Lovey-Dovey." It's sickening, it's nauseating. The real love is a nourishment, it strengthens your soul. The ordinary love only

feeds the ego, not the real you but the unreal you. The unreal always feeds the unreal, remember, and the real feeds the real.

As Osho puts it.

Let there be a nonphysical connection. Get to know why someone was brought into your life. What does he or she need to teach you? What are you supposed to teach this person? Talk to each other. Stop trying to attach yourself to another person because that's not real love.

Athlete's Tip: Know that to make any relationship or dating experience work, you must first know who you are! Understand that you will never begin to experience love or truly appreciate someone if you don't feel this way about yourself. Figure out your baggage before trying to become one with another. Don't use your relationships as an opportunity to cover up, run away, or hide from what *is*. Know that anyone you make a part of your life situation are an *addition to*. He or she should not be the reason you eat or sleep. That is not real.

Addition:
- The action or process of adding something to something else.
- A person or thing added or joined, typically to improve something.

Personally, No!

Taking things personally will only leave you personally hurt. Understand that people do things based on what they've been through, where they come from, and who they think they are. For example, the time Wade and I spent together. The reality of it is it didn't matter who Wade decided to date after his ex; he was going to compare the two men to each other. I could've been Jason, Sam, or Thomas; Wade would've still made it his business to try and recreate his previous experience with another. It was nothing personal toward me.

> **Side Note: There is a more significant problem here. People tend to believe that because they have gone through certain things in life, they have some sort of excuse to act out in careless ways, and that's not the case. While it's great to have people there for you, no one should have put up with your emotional distress. It's unfair. Insecure men and women—your insecurities are just that, your insecurities. No one should have to pay the price because you feel as though you are incompetent in some area of your life. You should spend some time alone and work through these things by yourself or with a paid professional.**

In situations where people are trying their best to insult, discredit, slut shame, or assault your character in the hopes of bringing you down, it's more about them making themselves look and feel superior—it's nothing personal. People can be spiteful and might say some awful things about you. But remember that people can only offend you if you give them the right to do so, and to give them that right, you must first acknowledge their existence.

THE POWER OF GOING AT IT ALONE.

The worst advice I believe you could ever get or give someone is "Prove everyone who has ever doubted you wrong." When someone tells you this, the person is subconsciously saying, "The people who said you cannot complete your goal(s) are the ones you need to keep in mind when you are putting in hard work, because those people matter to you the most. And if you don't prove them wrong, you're a failure, just as they said you were."

You see, it's the worst advice ever. Proving someone wrong is a waste of your time. If someone doesn't believe in you, why would you allow that person free access to your mind and emotions? You're inspired to work harder because someone told you that you cannot do something? That's not a happy or healthy way to live. If people don't believe in you, simply allow them to carry on about their day and their lives. No comment from you is needed. Do not devote your hard work to someone who doesn't see greatness in you. However, when you don't know better, you don't do better. Taking things like this personal will have you in a full-out war, hurling insults back to people simply because you feel/think you must prove a point. Don't allow anyone who doesn't believe in you a free opportunity to have a seat at your table.

Most of the time, when people tell you that you cannot achieve or accomplish something, it's because they themselves cannot achieve or accomplish it. "You will never amount to anything" always tends to come from those who have never amounted to anything or who will never amount to anything themselves. Again, you cannot take it personal. Your success or your will to succeed will make others feel insufficient in their current endeavors, and your success doesn't even have to be in terms of material achievements or money.

Success could be the way you love or how genuinely

happy you make yourself. Someone somewhere might see this and start to feel as if you think you are better than others. Simply because you are genuinely happy and have joy in your life. But know that this is an act of their own insecurities. You do not need to show up to this potential argument. If you are happy with yourself and love yourself, you know what this is about; you no longer need to prove anything to anyone. Smile and carry on. The same applies to someone cheating on you.

"How could you do this to me?" "How could you hurt me like this?" is what's asked once one finds out their partner has stepped out of their relationship, and the answer is simple: your lover wasn't thinking about you. Within the moment of infidelity, people are only worried about capturing or re-capturing a feeling that they feel is missing. Yes, a feeling! They aren't considering the possibility of hurting you, or potentially ruining the relationship they have.

Though there are a ton of articles and books that outline how to keep a man (or woman), you cannot keep what doesn't want to be kept. There is nothing you can do to prevent someone from stepping out on you, hard truth, but facts. You can be a great pleaser. You can be overly ambitious. You can be drop-dead gorgeous. You can be Beyoncé. If a man or a woman doesn't feel personally fulfilled within themselves, they will constantly look and explore others.

Instead of taking this moment like this, or any dating experience for that matter, personally, understand that there is a lack of some sort within his or herself that needs to be work on it. It has nothing to do with who you are, how you look, how much money you do or don't have, or what you bring to the table.

I've personally gone through a situation where I found out a guy that I took time to get to know had gone back to sleep with his ex. However, I forgave him, and over the years, I came to understand just why he did what he did. Not wanting to be back in a committed relationship with his Ex, he merely missed how his Ex made him feel, and because I am who I am, to many I am not what others are used to, nothing personal. I take it as a compliment.

Athlete's Tip: From your personal life to your professional life, people are going to take digs at you, talk about you, or make fun of you. Who cares? Let sleeping dogs lie.

Journal Entry

September 5, 2010
7:30 am

Dear Someone,

My relationships with my family & friends—I would say that it's okay, things can be better, but I can't help feeling like I am different from them. I don't know why, but my love for them is all the same. I love them all the same, and I forgive my mother's childish behavior. I forgive RF & TK for talking about me. But it's like it can happen at any time, so I just don't get into it with them. But I feel like I've done some wrong things to my mother and my sister, talking about them. I feel bad for that, I really do, and I feel like they are my family and I'm better than that, but I guess I was just mad. At this time, if you would forgive me for that, blood is thicker than water, and sometimes I can't help but feel like I just want to get up and leave them but not on a bad note. I don't want anyone to think or feel as though I'm doing it just because of my windfall, and I wouldn't want anyone to do it to me. But I need out of here and on with my life. Overall, I'm happy. Only thing I'm not happy about is my money problem. It could be better.

November 22, 2013
8:10 pm

I know God has a reason for everything that he put me through and sometimes I know I may cause some things for myself. And I'm fine with that. I may not be every person's flavor of great. But I'm not going to give up everything that I have and worked for, like I'm not giving it up! Each and every day there just are some things that I know I can't go to everyone for. They don't have to face anything that I go through and they are not trying to do anything that I'm trying to do with my life. I will give my last to the people I love, but the people I love will not do the same for me. If I continue giving my last, what will I have for myself and the things I have planned for me? When speaking of making sacrifices, I've made a ton. I've been places people didn't even want me to be. I've noticed when it comes to my lifestyle, not everyone agrees with it (not talking about being gay), and I'm fine with that. I respect everyone, even the more airheaded dick head. But I will not sacrifice everything for a temporary position. Again, I know God put me here for a reason, and it amazes me the people who believe they have something over my head. People love to feel like they've done major things for me, and I know everyone may feel that way about me. But it's not true. I've helped a lot, but no one sees that.

Part Three
YOU'RE THE ONLY ONE STANDING IN YOUR WAY

Chapter 5
BELIEVE IN YOU AND EVERYTHING YOU ARE!

The difference between those of us who "make it" and those who don't is our belief system, the belief that anything is possible and that we can do whatever the hell we want if we try.

It doesn't matter where you come from or your lack of schooling, resources, or any other excuse we may conjure up. Not to compare anyone but, chances are there's someone, somewhere who has been less fortunate than you and I yet has managed to make it out of whatever hellhole they were in, due to believing they could. Take me, for instance. I couldn't have any other odd stacked against me. I mean, I grew up a poor, introverted, black, gay man whose mom died when he was nineteen, missed out on his childhood, been mentally abused. Who had to drop out of high school, who then dropped out of college, and the list goes on. My situation could've gotten worst, but I decided and believed that something more, than what was, could happen.

Side Note: At sixteen, because I had to take care of myself, I was working a full-time job

at McDonald's while trying to attend High School. School started at 7:30 AM, and I would arrive home at 12:00 AM the night before; the McDonald's I worked at was inside BWI Airport, and my school, Edmondson Westside High School, was over in West Baltimore. So, it was hard, but I had to make it work considering I needed school supplies, clothes, and lunch. I was late every morning to school, and I never did homework; I never had the time. Just thinking about this makes me super emotional because getting an education wasn't even a priority.

After the school year came to an end, I wasn't surprised to see that I'd failed. From there, I dropped out of school and enrolled in Job Corps, where I received my GED within six months. Then from there I had to steal my Moms Social Security Number to enroll in Baltimore City Community College. She was afraid that the school would ruin her credit, so she told me she couldn't be the guardian on my FASFA application. However, I spent three years at BCCC before finally dropping out and moving to New York.

The significant difference between this "around-the-way" kid and countless others like me is I'm not afraid to believe in who I am or what I want. I know It's possible, and because of it I am now an author and, on my way, to be the owner of a pretty dope lifestyle company that I created.

Whether you're transgender, nineteen, or thirty-five, a Muslim, Mexican, or a Black Jew, it does not matter. You can have whatever you want in life if you believe. We all have odds stacked against us. We all come from a place of

BELIEVE IN YOU AND EVERYTHING YOU ARE!

oppression in some way, but what I have come to learn is poverty breeds creativity. "Ghetto is nothing but Creativity that hasn't been stolen yet," said writer Nezarial Scott on the hypocritical commercialization and commodification of black American fashion, vernacular, slang, culture, and livelihood.

Having less than is not a struggle, it's an opportunity for you to realize (1) you don't need a ton of stuff for you to be who you want to be, and (2) the lighter your load, the quicker you can get up and go. Coming from low-income housing, as I have, you're judged—sometimes made fun of, as if you don't have the ability to operate like some of your peers, but if you look closely, you'll see that that's my power. If I can accept the fact that my struggles are just obstacles in disguise, which were given to me so that I can see just how smart, creative, and crafty I really am, I win. Having to work ten times harder than the next person isn't a bad thing; it merely makes me ten times more willing, more dedicated, and able to succeed in whatever I do. People who were born into money never had to worry about stretching ten dollars until the next payday. Which means they never had to rely on pure creativity to get them out of sticky situations.

Don't get me wrong, struggles aren't the best when they're happening, but if you are aware after you've made it through, you do learn something new about yourself. When your back is up against the wall, you show yourself just what you're made of; I love moments like that. Remember: poverty breeds creativity. Know that everything you've been through has happened to you for a reason.

#WARDBODY

While writing this book, I may have asked myself a billion times, "Antoine, do you think people will get what you are doing? Do you think this book would sell? Do you believe people will feel and understand what you are saying with WardBody?" These doubts circulated in my mind continuously, and the truth is I don't know. I don't know if this book will sell, I don't know if people will get it. However, what I do know is I'm choosing to start with what I believe in and letting the rest follow. I believe in what I am creating, I believe in my writing, and I believe in myself, and that is more than enough for me.

WardBody exists because I want it to, because I live this lifestyle, and I've noticed how much my life has changed by simply making a decision and repeatedly acting on it. This book exists because I wanted to read a piece about a black gay man who followed his dreams and who has dealt with some of the things I've faced. A man who come from where I do, who sexuality is the same as mine. Someone who has witness abandonment and insecurities, yet, prosper. I wrote this book because I wanted to be the representation that I sought after when I was child.

> There is a certain delusional quality that all successful people must have. You must believe that something different than what has happened, can happen.
>
> – *Will Smith*

I'd never done this before, and this is the real reason behind my self-doubt or me questioning myself. I'd never even played sports before, yet I am building an athlete-like lifestyle brand that is, in a sense, constructed around how athletes think and operate. Who told me I could do this? Furthermore, I realized my life—better yet, our lives—are much like those of physical athletes. Instead of training for a challenge that happens every four years like the Olympics, we work, and we strive every year, some of us every day, becoming smarter and more skilled in our professions and practices. I didn't need to step into an actual boxing ring to learn how to become more calculating—although I do know my way around one. However, my point is if you look closely, you'll see that life could be a UFC match where you are trying to knock out old habits or conquer a self-defeating mindset. Our lives could also be like a game of football, needing to depend on our team (friends and family) more to score touchdowns (goals).

I don't have to play sports to think and function like someone on a hockey field or a tennis court, and neither do you. Winning is a mental game. Greatness is how you think, how you train, and how you pick yourself up after what looks like a defeat.

When I decided to move to New York I didn't ask my father; I told him what I was going to do. Same with going to and dropping out of college. I had to start believing in myself to make my own decisions and trust that I wouldn't steer myself in the wrong direction. I did a few times, and it was well worth it.

> *Athlete's Tip:* When you are starting out or taken on a new goal and doing something you have never done before, know that self-doubt is normal, and it's the most honest thing you can offer yourself. Life has a way of looking you in the face and asking you, "Are you sure you want this? How bad do you want this?" and it's up to you to prove to yourself just how much you want what you say you want. Believe in yourself, even

when you don't know how to, even when you feel like it's impossible.

Confucius once said, "He who says he can and he who says he can't are both usually right." There's a redemptive power that making a choice has, rather than feeling like you're an effect of all the things that are happening. Make a decision; you must decide: What's it going to be? Who are you going to be? How are you going to do it?

— *Will Smith*

More Pain, Please!

I will bet you one billion dollars (which I don't have) that you will learn more on the days you call bad than on the days you call good. Would you bet me? Jim Afremow wrote in his book *The Champion's Mind: How Great Athletes Think, Train, and Thrive*:

> Our society has conditioned us to believe there should be no discomfort in life, and when we are uncomfortable, we think something is terribly wrong. As such, we all tend to resist that which is initially uncomfortable. Instead, something is terribly right when we're challenged to grow stronger.

A life with no pain, depression, or discomfort and no reason to sacrifice what you love for what you want? Sounds like the perfect life, would you agree? I don't. There would be no growth without struggles, and no pain means a life with no change or challenges, no happily-ever-afters.

BELIEVE IN YOU AND EVERYTHING YOU ARE!

Call me crazy, but I've fallen in love with my ruin, and I realized that pain really isn't what we believe it to be.

For example, everything you asked for, it's given to you—it's law—whether you pray about it, ask the Universe for it, or chant to Buddha. You will always get what you—physically or mentally—ask for, this also goes for what you *do not* ask for, but that's another story for another book. Furthermore, from the time when you asked for what you wanted to the time to when it's given, a process began. Maybe you noticed, or perhaps you didn't. However, you start going through a stream of what seemed like problems, pain, or conflict, but in hindsight, are lessons that are required. During the moments of conflict and pain, you began learning what's needed of you for you to have that which you asked for or wanted.

Allow me to simplify that. If you voice out or pray, "I want to be taken seriously," you'll notice in almost every area of your life situation how much people don't take you seriously. You'll also begin to experience moments where it seems like you got the complete opposite of what you asked for, but again, what's happening is you are being offered moments to learn. You want others to take you seriously, but you don't know what being taken seriously entails? How do people act who are taken seriously? What makes others take them seriously? You'll discover these answers and more during your process.

The same with love. You've asked God for it, you prayed to Jesus about it, and you finally scored a relationship. Then, around month seven, you start to realize that things aren't what you expected them to be, but what's wrong? He said all the right things to win you over; she's been down for you since day one. What could be the problem? You realize that there isn't a problem; it's just, sweet words and someone holding you down isn't love. You've started to feel as if those two things just aren't enough anymore. You learn that these are acts of love but not love within itself, but how could God give you what you asked for, how dare Jesus listen to you?

The problem is, you never offered yourself space between where you were and your wedding day. This space consists typically of two to three people who you believed wasted your time. They bought you pain, unhappiness, and insecurities, but what they also did was show you, with each individual experience, what real love is or what it could potentially be. They helped you define love or redefine love. You asked to be in love, but you never had a definition of what love meant to you. So, who is wasting whose time?

Pain consists of the lessons you need to learn to attain your desired goal, and the process is inevitable. Pain lies in between where you are and where you want to be. The goal is to accept all that is or all that will be, becoming a servant to the struggles that have manifest in your life. If you accept the BS that is your process, pain cannot pain you. I understand that you may get tired or grow restless with your life situation at times but keep in the back of your mind that to get any new position, you must first go through training; at work, in the gym, within your relationship. Personally, that's all pain is: *the process of preparation* and by surrendering to your process of training, you eliminate the thoughts and emotions that ego wants you to feel—the idea that "I am suffering."

I asked the Universe, "Universe, can I inspire people to chase their dreams and to get shit done?" The Universe told me, "Chase yours; you get shit done." Okay, bet. I then stated, "Universe, I really want to be my own boss and run my own company." The Universe said, "Build one." Okay, **#WardBody**. Finally, I said, "We as black gay men need more representation." and the Universe replied, "Be it." and within moments, I began going through the process and soon understanding just why I've been through everything I have. To build or to create what I want to be a part of, I had to first go through it myself. How can one preach to others to **#GETSHITDONE** if he has never done anything, has never been through anything? My life situation set me up to be the Boss I want to be. If I am willing to constantly give up what I have for what I want and accept all that I must, pain can't "pain me."

I have fully accepted that money will be an issue for me and that I may need help from loved ones to bail me out occasionally. I am an entrepreneur, or soon to be one, which means every cent I earn needs to go into what I want to create. I have accepted the fact that I will not be able to hang out and run the town as much as I want to in my twenties, and I fully understand what I need to do to get where I want to be. I am dedicated to my process, and because of this acceptance, there aren't any issues.

Money, or the lack thereof, is no longer an issue. Do you understand? Surrender—and again, by surrender, I mean accept—to what is and allow it to be. I now know that pain doesn't happen; it's created. The feeling of pain is illustrated by our wants and what ego says we need. If you're aware of what you're asking for or what your ego demands, you'll then be able to understand why you are suffering or why you are in pain. A man who wants nothing feels nothing. Pain is inevitable; it is part of our journey and evolution. It's okay to feel things, to go through things, and to go without things; everything happens for a reason.

Don't try to resist what is, allow yourself to sit with it, be in it, and feel it. It's an integral step on your path.

Anyone who wants to experience an all-time high, or feel a tremendous sense of joy, will experience all-time lows. The goal here is to discover the hidden gems in your ruin. What are you supposed to apply your life lessons to? How will you use the pain that's been offered to you, for your greater good? You are not suffering because someone doesn't like you; there's no mystical creature trying to stop your shine. Ms. Minaj isn't stopping your bag. The Universe—or God, Allah, or Buddha—is simply holding you accountable to what you said you want. It's a privilege to be in pain, and it's a blessing to know what to do with it and feeling pain doesn't mean you are losing. It means you are growing.

> *Athlete's Tip:* If you have ever completed any form of physical training, the next day you probably felt aches and pains all over your body. These aches and sharp pains signify that you got something done. Everyday Athletes understand that much of their success depends on how well they handle non-injurious pain, soreness, tiredness, and discomfort. We also know that body aches and pains are a necessary part of improving and magnifying our physical and mental performance. They are an essential part of the training process. We know that intense discomfort is often the price we pay for personal greatness.

Practice Detachment

I believe it's natural to feel as if we need to hold on to things. Whether it's jewelry someone who passed away has given you, a pair of shoes you wore to prom back in 2006, or even the china set that was part of your wedding five years ago. It's natural to want to hold onto these things because they serve a purpose in your life and they are of value and somehow make you, you.

When either a moment or a person brings you joy or hurt, we cling to it, making that thing or being a part of our identity. For example, someone who graduated from college will consider him or herself a college graduate, a woman who had a baby will know herself as a mom, and a man who owns his own company will know himself as a boss, but the truth is that these are roles.

Ego tends to equate having with being: I have, therefore I am. And the more I have, the more I am.

– Eckhart Tolle

The roles we play, the things we own, and the people we may know do not make us who we are. Being a mom, a college student or a boss is merely an experience that helps us create ourselves, yet these things aren't who we are. Personally speaking, I don't identify with anything outside of my inner self because the truth is who I am, can only be felt. Even after I finish writing this book and I go on to market it, I don't plan to call myself an author. That's just too serious for me; no one owes me any respect, nor am I demanding that you look at me in a new light. I am Antoine Ward, a guy who made it out of hard circumstances, who now lives his life in a way that he appreciates and decided to write about it. I am no god—only my god. I am not an influencer, a public figure, or any other label one may give oneself. I sincerely enjoy being "just Antoine."

The accumulation of stuff we collect, over time, begin to act as an anchor and weigh us down. I had a friend who lived in New York but traveled back home to Baltimore almost every weekend—we used to joke that she was living two lives, but that's how it is when you aren't ready to let go. You keep one foot here and the other there, it took her some time to feel as if New York was her home finally.

Before my dear friend made the ultimate decision to let go of everything that seemed to be helping hold herself back, it was like the Universe was testing her to see if she wanted what she said she wanted. She had a car—this car serves as a prime example of an anchor and the reason I write this. This car created more problems than anything else in her life during this time of transition. I remember telling her, "Please get rid of this thing you need to let it go."

> **Side Note: If you dream of being successful and you are just embarking on your journey, try your best not to tie up all your funds in things like monthly subscriptions and recurring bills. That is, if something is not needed to help manifest your ultimate dream, instead invest in things that will offer you a return: for example, books, information, seminars, or places, and things that will help your business, image, or idea boom. Trying to start a business or a company requires money. Paying for things like car insurance, car notes, the latest iPhone every year, or new shoes every week is just not smart. Not to count anyone's money, but your checks are required**

for more pressing things. Stop buying and start investing.

    I could see how much of an investment this car was, and she needed a lighter load for the journey she was about to embark on. This car literally served as a helping hand for my friend to get from point A to B in her life, and now at point B life required a new form of transportation.

    Every week, it seemed like there was a problem with this car. Once someone made a mistake and got a key stuck in the transmission; another time the car faced impoundment, this all happened within the same year— maybe two to three months apart. My friend than even tried to bring the car to New York, but once she got it here, she had another set of unique problems. From paying for daily/monthly fees for parking to having to find parking, it was a lot. Until one day she finally sold it, and life began to make much more sense. But something happened to my friend—she didn't stop at getting rid of the car. She started to let go of almost everything she owned, even close friendships because she had finally realized what needed to happen for her to become more of herself.

    Your journey is your journey, and if you are someone who wants to be great, you must make great sacrifices. Not everything you've acquired from age twenty-one to twenty-five can come along with you at twenty-six, and more importantly, why would you want it? As I stated earlier, trying to keep things the same is how you create pain and needless suffering for yourself. Your car, your house, your spouse, or any other prize possession you may obtain will not make you who you are, and somewhere down the line, that thing or person will begin to bring you more problems than joy. Evolution will always win.

Letting go does not always mean *to get rid* of; it can also mean *to let be*. When we let be—with compassion—things come and go on their own. You don't have to force it, and at times you don't have to announce it. As Jack Kornfield says, "Every new level of your life is going to require a new level of you. From how you think, to how you respond, to what you invest your time into." What has happened in your life has happened; accept it and let it be.

After my mom passed away, my siblings believed that holding on to our mom's ashes and old photos were somehow showing great respect and cherishing our mother's life. Throwing anniversary parties, candlelight visuals, and releasing balloons; I didn't agree with it, but it's what we do. However, growing to understand that we all grieve differently, and that death is a process; what my siblings didn't see was how much pain and hurt they were causing themselves.

For me too personally live happier and healthier, I had to let my mom die, in theory, and I had to allow her to, mentally and physically, rest in peace. I grew to a point where I realized that the death of my mother could no longer help me with where I was in my life, and it was best that I let her go. I no longer wanted to feel helpless or sorry for myself and what I've gone through, and I no longer wanted to be a victim of my life situation.

The thought of my mom not existing in this realm no longer makes me want to cry. I am not angry about it, as I once was, nor do I care to hold on to any memorabilia of hers. It does nothing for me. The only thing my mother's death can offer me right now in life is an excuse to blame others for what I do not have and who I am not. I will never have another Mom for as long as I live, and I am 100 percent okay with this. I now know that on the other side of what is, is real life.

To help you let be, I have listed seven tips that have helped me live happier and healthier. Take what you need and try applying these tips to your life situation.

1. Always Forgive.

Allowing oneself to forgive is one of the many ways you offer yourself inner joy and inner peace. Forgiveness is about releasing the anxiety or anger you may have built up toward someone or something, that seems to be holding you in a space of misery or discomfort. Forgiving isn't about letting one off the hook or hearing the words "I'm sorry." It's not trying to forcefully make someone own up to their responsibilities in causing pain or suffering, but instead, it's simply coming to terms with an event or experience and allowing oneself to grow.

2. You control no one, and no one controls you.

You cannot change another person, so don't waste your time and energy trying. Don't try to jump through hoops to prove your loyalty or your worth for others to see. Don't think, "If I do everything for everyone, they'll never get mad at me." Wrong! Lead with who you are first, without ego, and if people become upset allow them to be.

3. Only worry about what you think of yourself.

People can describe parts of you, they can mention how you responded to certain things and how you handled certain situations, but they cannot tell you who you are. That is only up to you. You can disagree with any allegation or personality trait that someone, from your mother to your office manager, tries to attach to your character. You have the last say on who you are, no matter how you handled a situation or what you said during an altercation.

4. Leave room for mistakes.

Mistakes are needed, and they will 100 percent happen to you, and you have the right to make them. You can misspell a word, you can send an email to the wrong person, or you can forget a piece of information. Keep your intentions pure and honest and accept that you've made a mistake when you realize you have.

5. Allow yourself to feel negative emotions.

When experiencing pain, loss, or suffering, allow yourself to feel it all. If you are sad, let yourself to be sad. Trying to ignore your negative emotions will extend your misery. A loss is a challenging experience, and it's okay to allow yourself to hurt. Let yourself feel and go through the grief process so that you can properly move forward.

6. Express yourself.

Not only are you allowed to have a voice, but you can use it. If you are uncomfortable, speak up! If you do not like how something is playing out or if you do not feel appreciated, speak up! Gone are the days when you sit quietly and take what's given. Be assertive—despite being told you seem angry—let the world and the people in it know just what you want and how you feel.

7. Run toward what scares you.
Head first, run and dive into what scares you. Fear holds you back from doing everything you want to do. It closes your mind to what can be and holds you in your comfort zone. Fear is self-doubt, and the more you allow it to exist, the more you put yourself in a mental prison. Fail fast, to learn lessons sooner, and continuously fail forward; do not be afraid of failing, and do not beat yourself up about it. Know what you don't know.

I am not what happened to me, I am what I choose to become.

– Carl Jung

Athlete's Tip: Failing to understand that sacrifice is mandatory can lead to a life filled with resentment and regret. Know that you cannot become the champ you desire to be if you are not willing to allow yourself to grow and leave a few people behind. He who wants to be great needs to occupy the space in which the opportunity he seeks is given. A lot of times these spaces are outside of your comfort zone and the city and state in which you grew up. As an Everyday Athlete, you owe it to yourself to see how great you are or can be. Take full responsibility for yourself and hold yourself accountable. Allow yourself to know that you are the only thing standing in your way – no one else.

Chapter 6
TRIP!

> As I release these frequencies, speak to me. Every low, foul listener please keep from me. As I release these frequencies.
>
> – Jhene Aiko

Jhene Aiko is one of my favorite artists, and her last album, *Trip*, was the inspiration for this chapter—hence, the chapter title. In Jhene's music, she speaks about balance, wholeness, frequency, awareness, and a ton of other things I connect with, on both an emotional and a spiritual level. This chapter is dedicated to getting to know oneself, the self that we do not see—the inner us. This chapter is more enlightened, more in tuned with self, than the others. Getting to know myself, I have been able to connect to the Universe that dwells inside of me, the Universe that is me. That may sound foreign to you hearing/reading this, but it's true.

#WARDBODY

Frequency Frequently

What is vibrational frequency, and how does one live off it? Vibrational frequency is a way to describe your overall state of being. Everything in the Universe contains energy that vibrates at different frequencies. Even things that look solid embody vibrational energy fields at the quantum level. This includes you yourself, trees, rocks, food, animals, oceans, sand, and the list goes on. And the way one lives off vibrational frequency, or energy, is by simply listening to oneself. Vibrational frequency is the reason I moved out of Baltimore, it's the reason many of my employers terminated me, and it's also the reason why in 2015 I cut off everyone I was friends with.

Pamela Dussault said it best in her 2012 article "The Benefits of Being in a Higher Vibration," for *Huffington Post*:

> Vibrational Frequency is the rate at which something occurs or is repeated over a period or in a given sample. We all vibrate energetically at a specific frequency:
>
> The lower your frequency, the denser your energy, and the more massive your problems seem. Here you may experience strong emotions and mental confusion or experience discomfort and pain in your physical body. Psychically, your energy is darker. You need to exert a great deal of effort to accomplish your goals. Overall, your life takes on a negative quality. The higher the frequency of your energy or vibration, the lighter you feel in your emotional, physical, and mental bodies. You experience greater peace, love, personal power, joy, and clarity. Your emotions are quickly dealt with, and you'll have little, if any,

pain or discomfort in your physical body. Your life flows with synchronicity, and you manifest what you desire with ease. Your energy is full of light, and overall your life takes on a positive quality.

When our energy is high or low, the Universe senses this and begin to offer us vibrational patterns that match our current vibrational frequency. For example, a bad day becomes a bad week, which then becomes a bad month. It's Law. When something horrible happens in our life, and we hold our focus on that bad thing, we then create a web that will universally spin and continue to match that matter in which we identify as bad.

Suppose you're dating, and your date tells you that he or she no longer has ties with their ex, they let you know that both parties have moved on completely. However, something recently happened that made you feel otherwise. Maybe you saw them chopping it up on twitter or the ex-texted him, and you just so happened to see the notification. So, you don't believe her just yet. What then happens is, you physiologically begin to create a space for his or her ex to exist—and because you are one with your emotions, *that which is like unto itself is drawn*.

You will notice the ex is everywhere. You'll realize someone in your social circle has strong ties with the ex, or you'll start having dreams about the two of them together. Maybe you'll start to notice how often the ex appears on your social media feed or timeline(s). All these things will begin to exist only to match your "I-know-something-is-going-on-here" frequency, even though your date could've been telling you the truth. Still, you gave your attention to what you did not want to happen, the Universe matched that and gave you what you asked for, again, it is law.

> Whatever you are giving your attention to causes you to emit a vibration, and the vibrations that you offer equal your asking, which equals your point of attraction.
>
> – *Ask and It Is Given*
> by Eshter and Jerry Hicks

    I have grown to live entirely off personal energy and vibrational frequency. Meaning, I listen with my body when occupying spaces or when I am in conversation with others. My eyes, my smile, and my hands have a unique way of letting me know when things are or aren't of my liking. Furthermore, my awareness and introduction of Vibrational frequency have been through the help of two close friends. From these individuals, I've learned not only are you responsible for the energy that you bring or dish out, but you are also responsible for the energy in which you surround yourself.

    I'd just enrolled in an online course at the New York Institute of Art and Design, where I began studying interior decorating. I'd also just started working as a sales assistant for a furniture showroom that specialized in custom upholstery and casework goods. So, not only was I studying how to design and decorate a space, but I was also getting hands-on experience; learning how to sell furniture and create it as well. At the time, I was even dating this awesome guy whom I'd become quite attracted to, and things seemed to be going well. Overall, my life situation was looking pretty good.

    Meanwhile, aside from all the greatness taking place in my life, I had two friends who were both going through a bit of a rough patch. One dealing with a breakup and had a hard time finding some self-respect for himself, while the other was very ambitious yet couldn't seem to catch a break or get the help she believed she needed. My two friends' depressions resulted in daily victim role-playing, crying, complaining, and drinking four to five days a week— because this was during the moment in my life when I was trying to prove to everyone and myself just how much of a friend I was. I was devoted to listening to every complaint, wiping every tear, and agreeing to every victimizing notion that both friends felt. "How could he do this to you? You gave him everything?" "Life is so hard. Why can't you have everything you asked for." and because I was so unaware as to how energy worked, depression soon enveloped me too.

It honestly took this situation for me to realize that misery has no boundaries. When someone is depressed, they attached themselves to the identity and commit to playing the down-and-out role. Because of the state of their emotions, they will not be able to assist their situation and say to their friends, "Hey, while I do appreciate you being here for me. I know my depressed state will begin to rub off onto you and I don't want to consume you with this energy overly. You are in a great place in your life, and I must deal with this my own, for now." The worst thing you can do when you are depressed is nothing. Hanging with my friends during their depression made me depressed. I forgot about how much I enjoyed my job, the things I was learning, and the person I was dating. My energy matched theirs completely, and we became one. I began complaining, crying, and drinking right along with the two of them.

Then a day came when I was inspired to take my energy back. During my time apart from my friends, I was reading a book—a book that has since become my favorite book and the blueprint for how I view my life situation. How I experience moments and people, and how I was able to realize that I am everything and nothing at the same time: A New Earth by Eckhart Tolle. Reading this book, I learned about pain bodies, role-playing, self-definition, projecting, and so much more—and as I read, something in his book made me go, *"Wow, this is happening to me right now."*

> A very common role is the one of victim, and the form of attention it seeks is sympathy or pity or others' interest in my problems, "me and my story." Seeing oneself as a victim is an element in many egoic patterns, such as complaining, being offended, outraged and so on. Of course, once I'm identified with a story in which I assigned myself the role of victim, I don't want it to end, and so, as every therapist knows, the ego does not want an end to its "problems" because they are part of its identity. If no one will listen to my sad story, I can tell it to myself in my head, over and over, and feel sorry for myself, and so have an identity as someone who is being treated unfairly by life or other people, fate or God. It gives definition to my self-image, makes me into someone, and that is all that matters to the ego.

I instantly became aware of what was happening with my friends, and I began to shift my gears. You see, the more I hung out with my friends, being there for them, basking in their depression, the more I was unconsciously giving them permission to be depressed, to play a victim as if someone or something had done something to them. However, they were both merely feeding off each other's victimized nature. With the two of them feeling as if they'd been done wrong in some way, they matched each other's vibrational pattern and began producing massive waves of depression, growing larger pain bodies, and affecting anyone who decided to occupy or share a space with them..

After undoing this moment in my life, I learned that my frequency began to vibrate a little higher than my friends', causing me to distance myself. I now know you must set boundaries. Oversharing of one's life situation is borderline disrespectful, especially if it's constant negativity. I am not saying you shouldn't share your thoughts, feelings, or news with your friends and loved ones. Negative stuff happens all the time; however, you do not have to continuously give that energy out or share every intricate detail with others—in person or on social media. That energy carries; it spreads. If you are depressed, try to work through what you feel by yourself first—because, honestly, in the end, you are the only one who can say when you've had enough. Then, when your emotions aren't running high or all over the place, you can include others. Lead with, "I'm informing you about what's going on in my life and the next step I need to take." Not, "I'm lost, I'm panicking, I don't know what to do next, help me—help me—help me." You should be able to discuss your issues with your friends and loved ones but be aware of your energy and the fact that everyone else in your circle could be dealing with something. You—and no one else—should have to go through certain (keyword *certain)* things alone. However, it would be best if you also respected what others may have going on.

If you are someone who wants to be in pain or wants to be depressed, I can sympathize with you, but I have nothing for you. We could discuss you being down and out one good time, and after that, you must find someone else to vent to. I used to believe that this made me a bad person, but I learned that if you do not draw your line, people will walk over you with their negativity, and I've reached a point in my life where I cannot allow that. Further, at some point, while dealing with depression, pain, or discomfort, you need to ask yourself: Am I resisting something in my life situation? Am I victimizing myself? Am I taking something that has nothing to do with me extremely personal? Alternatively, do I want/need some attention? Someone who doesn't want to be down-and-out will choose not to be.

How does one raise one's vibrational frequency?

Become conscious of your thoughts.
What you think, say, do, or feel becomes your reality. Every single thought that comes into your head has an impact on you and how you live. If it doesn't promote the person you want to be or the life you want to live, ditch it.

Try looking for the collateral beauty in mayhem.
After every war, there's an opportunity to start anew. Anything that has happened or is happening to you make it your mission to look for the lesson that is being-taught. Accept the war that is going on, and after the dust settles, choose to see how beautiful life is about to become.

Be conscious of the foods you eat.
Pay attention to how eating certain foods makes your body feel. Some foods vibrate at high frequencies and others lower—asparagus has a high vibration, as do pineapples. Big Macs don't vibrate at all. If you are consuming foods covered with chemicals and pesticides or foods found within plastic packaging, they will leave you vibrating lower. Consume good-quality organic produce, food as nature intended it, and feel the high vibrations disseminate throughout your body.

Practice meditation.
Find someplace quiet and sit in a comfortable position, close your eyes, and breathe in and out. Too often, we rush through our days with scattered brains, leaving us in states of anxiety and stress. Meditation helps calm our spirits and puts us in peaceful states of mind. Ten to thirty minutes of meditation a day can change our days, weeks, and years.

Be grateful.
No matter where you come from or where you are going, what you have or don't have, be grateful. You are alive, and you can work to have what you want. You are no longer in a place where you used to be. If you are reading this, you've come a long way.

Be kind and do the right thing.
My dad always said, "If it's not from the heart, don't give it to me." Giving and being of service to others—if you can—without expecting anything in return heightens your frequency. Abundance is a high vibration.

Get your blood pumping.
Vibration requires movement: the more you move, the better your vibrations. The happier you feel, the more you will draw happy experiences to yourself because you are operating at a different frequency.

The universal Law of Attraction is that you draw to yourself the essence of whatever you predominantly think. Have you ever wondered why you attract certain types of people or life situations? It's your frequency. Drawing the same kind of man or woman, behavior patterns in friends and family, or jobs is not a coincidence; it's law. How you feel and what you think about yourself sets the stage for what you attract. If you feel insecure or believe you are not good enough, you will welcome people into your existence that help you bring these thoughts and feelings, you have about yourself, to life; it's law.

> *Athlete's Tip:* Become severely aware of your source. Learn the ways and possibilities that you could potentially hurt another or, better yet, hurt yourself. Learn and understand how you vibrate and what you are predominantly giving your attention? The overall goal for the Everyday Athlete is to be joyful. Can you find the joy in you at this moment? Understand that life does not have to be long; it merely needs to be lived—in quality, not luxury. Believe in doing the right thing, always. Tell the people who listen to your sob stories, "Thank you for taking time out of your day to listen to me, and I apologize for the energy I gave you." Educate yourself and raise your frequency.

Ascension—A Conversation with Self

Using your mind to bend metal or to drop full stadiums on your enemy, like Magneto I believe is the most significant power one could ever have, but aside from that, the power of being self-aware is cool too. Not realizing the potential, I possess to create my reality, grow my awareness, and understand that it's solely up to me to make decisions about who I want to be, these chapters would not exist, nor would the lifestyle that I live. Myself and many like me are the prime examples of what your life situation could look like if you allow yourself to become. Self-awareness is the conscious knowledge of one's character, feelings, motives, and desires. In my opinion, the richest and most fulfilled men and women in this world have nothing but a sense of who they are.

To know why you do what you do, where your feelings and thoughts steam from, why you respond to lost or love the way you do, how you feel, and to have the ability to voice those feelings while knowing you are the creator of your heaven or hell should be **#Goals!** Self-awareness is humbly knowing *"I have all the power I need."* It's knowing *"I am enough."* It also means, you are putting your focus on:

- what you are thinking;
- what you are speaking;
- how you are acting;
- how you are feeling;
- what you are eating;
- how you are reacting;
- what (and who) you are attracting;
- how you make decisions;
- what you are hiding;
- what patterns you see in your life; and
- how your body is responding.

Awareness is to examine oneself. It means understanding what motivates you and whether, or not, your motives or intentions match up with your conscious decisions. When you began to answer the above questions with clarity and honesty, you begin to act on WardBody's philosophy. Meaning you have begun to awaken the higher faculty within you that is self-awareness or consciousness. This then results in building or creating *a new earth*, a new earth that is you.

(See the introduction for WB's philosophy.)

in addition to being self-aware, there is a skill that we, as beings, all have. Moreover, if we were to develop this skill more, we'd offer ourselves the opportunity to make more confident, and accurate decisions about our well-being. Studies show women are more in tune with this skill than men, but, like some men, some women choose not to use (or listen to) this skill. This skill is intuition, also known as the feeling in your "gut."

> The rational mind is a faithful servant, and the intuitive mind is a sacred gift. We have created a society that honors the servant and has forgotten the gift.
>
> – *Albert Einstein*

Intuition is a perception that happens in the present; it's swift, but this momentary perception could be swept away by cognitive analysis. In our society, based on technology and rational thought, we often overthink our initial response. When you develop the faculty of intuition, your sense of "effortless knowing" will increase, and your sense of struggle will lessen. You will no longer be a mass of contradictions because you will always know. Your past experiences shape your intuition and your existing knowledge. Listening to the feeling in your gut, you'll begin to experience the sense of knowing things before you know them. By growing our intuition, we are then able to sense when we are in danger, or if someone is telling a lie; you will know when something is entirely off and just not right.

There will be an easiness to things because when your

intuition is working well, you'll have plenty of prana vayu—the fundamental energizing force. It is the inward-moving vital energy that governs respiration and reception, allowing us to take in everything from air and food to impressions and ideas. You'll be able to use your intuition to embrace others and to know them, their real selves. You will start to feel a sense of oneness; a connectedness rather—to your source. *"I am learning the Language of the World, and everything in the world is beginning to make sense to me...even the flight of the hawks," he said to himself. And, in that mood, he was grateful to be in love. When you are in love, things make even more sense, he thought."* said Paulo Coelho. Sharpening your intuitive skill is an act of self-love, grow the love for self and know the language of the world.

All things are the manifestation of one thing only. Love!

Before noticing just how disconnected from my source I was, and before understanding the importance of listening to the inner voice that resided in me—that was me—I felt as if there'd been two people who lived in me who were at war with one another.

I witnessed moments where my internal and external selves weren't fond of each other, resulting in a mass of self-contradiction. I noticed this fight with Self when I became aware of the right thing to do but ignored doing it. For example, when I first decided to lose weight and take ownership of my body yet did nothing to get the results I wanted. Further, when I knew not to trust certain people yet stayed connected to them; which resulted in drama-filled fallouts. Our intuition to do the right thing is always alive and very potent, yet we ignore it, causing unnecessary issues. The gut feeling is real and your inner self knows best. You know, exactly, what you need to do, listen to yourself!

> **Side Note: The moment you decide to listen to yourself, you can always feel what's real. I know this has been the case for me. Now, as an adult, I can forever feel when someone is faking it until they make it and not being honest.**

Not being one with, or conscious of, your source tends to transform small mistakes into huge problems, if overlooked continuously. For example, you visit your local coffee shop, the shop is busy, but you managed to get your order in. You ask for a small iced coffee to enjoy on a sunny day. Ten to fifteen minutes go by, and you receive a small hot coffee. You are clearly aware and can see that this is a mistake, but you do not speak up. You accept what the barista gave you because she has a ton of different orders, and you don't want to cause a scene or take her attention away from what she's doing to correct this minor or honest mistake. You think that by accepting this mistake, you are somehow understanding, not pushy, and not making a big deal of the situation, but deep down, you had your heart set on that iced coffee, being as how it's 95 degrees outside. However, you suck it up, and you accept what the barista has given you.

This incident has happened to me repeatedly. Also, please note that this situation has nothing to do with coffee! More so, this is about not listening to oneself when yourself is telling you to stop overlooking and accepting what life feels it's going to give you, despite what you asked for. Neglecting to address small issues, such as coffee, leads to a road of internal arguments and more significant problems; how you do one thing is how you do all things. If we're willing to accept something as small as a beverage how will one begin to voice or speak up about boundaries that their family or friends tend to overstep? It might sound crazy, and seem like there's a significant difference, but there isn't.

Therefore, now, as an adult, I do not do anything I genuinely do not want to do. I cannot accept what something or someone is giving me; I can only allow what I asked (paid) for.

Further, the main lesson you'll need to learn here is how to tell the difference between your intuition and your ego. If not aware, your ego will allow you to believe your insecurities are your intuition.

Your ego is the voice in your head that wants you to be liked; it wants you to prove yourself to people, be in control, and provoke. Ego creates your thoughts that talk shit and entitlement. These thoughts do a great job of keeping you safe from possible ridicule. Intuition, however, is your inner wisdom—the feeling in your gut that alarms you when you are in danger. It's the subtle knowing that happens without you ever having any idea why you know it. Intuition is much softer than ego, and it has a way of enlightening you.

Over time, if you do not begin listening, your intuition will start to create internal resistance about where you are. You'll have a strong feeling that you need to be doing this other thing and the more you ignore it, everything you don't want will begin to manifest in your life experience. When you don't break up with someone you know you need to, the arguments get worst, and the fights escalate. When you know, you need to stand up for yourself and let your father know just how you feel, but you push it off, the relationship will soon be over altogether. Have you notice this in your life situation? How many times have you been aware of what you needed to do, but didn't do it? How did things end?

> **Side Note: I believe this is one of the main reasons why many individuals become addicted to drugs, alcohol, or maybe even sex. These individuals need to forget. They want to shut up the voice in them telling them, "You know you need to do that." "You know you need to do this." The last thing an addict want to hear is someone or something telling them what they already know they need to do; this can also lead to suicide. The voice that lives in all of us can sometimes become too much to bear if you don't want to listen, and all we would like to do is silence it. Again, the goal here isn't to silence it. It's to listen up!**

All of us on the face of this earth know what we need to do to live how we see fit—our guts tell us, and the only thing worse than our knowing is knowing yet doing nothing about it. Which then causes depression.

Imagine someone knocking on your door and you being lazy laying across your sofa, yelling, "Who is it?" yet you don't bother getting up to go see. You ask again, "Who is it?" and again there's no answer. However, the knocking continues over and over and over, repeatedly. The knocking on your imaginary door possess as your intuition and your external self constantly yells out, "Who is it?" The mission is to get up and go see. If you do not listen to what yourself is either telling you what you must do, need to do, or what you should be doing, you will be the reason for your hell.

Distinguish your impulses from your intuition. Here are some suggestions to help you discern real intuitive information from wishful thinking.

1. True intuition is quiet and calm. It's never pushy, grandiose, obsessive, or manipulative. It does not advise us on what other people should do but only on what we should act on or do.
2. True intuition is supportive and directive, never judgmental, critical, shaming, or blaming. Beware of your ego: a message or a voice that appeals to the ego, to the personality, or to stature in the world is not coming from intuition.
3. Intuition does not lecture, explain, or elaborate in detail.
4. You get simple, direct information. Beware of the ego, which gives you logical arguments and reasons why you can't follow your hunches.
5. Real intuition always has your best interests at heart.

Make a conscious effort to sit in solitude, meditate, and be informed. Let yourself tell you a thing or two.

Athlete's Tip: Intuitive thoughts may give you warnings that challenge and divert you from a path you have begun to follow. Intuition is never misleading and should be seen as messages—omens rather, *or the way of the world*. The challenge to the rational mind is to accept intuition and use it as though you've been given a gift of direction and grace. Following your intuition requires you to love and to trust in yourself.

The payoff for listening to oneself is a *happier and healthier* life situation, I would know. Being aware of the decisions we make and the reasons we make them leaves no room for self-violation. Being self-aware helps us manifest inner joy, which then creates light—light that others will notice and search for it within themselves. Again, this is manifesting WardBody's philosophy.

Jukai—The Impact of Creating Space

In the formal ceremony known as *jukai*, a Zen practitioner openly receives and acknowledges the sixteen Bodhisattva precepts as a continuous path in his or her life. (A Bodhisattva is a person who's able to reach nirvana but delays doing so out of compassion to save suffering beings.) *Jukai* is made up of *ju*, which means "receiving/granting," and *kai*, which means "precepts." At a deeper level, *ju* means "to open a space within the core of our being to what is natural and true." It is perhaps more like "making" a space in which the precepts can manifest as what is natural. So, in this sense, *ju* opens to what is.

"Experience the gap" is a phrase I learned back when I began meditating. It means to experience the silent space between thoughts. This space is also where you allow your emotions, your feelings, and both your physical and nonphysical self the opportunity to all catch up with one another. In this section of the book, I would like to talk about the space, both mental and physical, that we must create to help grow our awareness, our self, and our vibrational frequency.

Meditating is hard for some, to sit for thirty minutes

to an hour, eyes closed, legs crossed, quiet, still, and focusing on one's breath? It can be challenging. Personally speaking, through this practice I've learned so many things, one being the importance of hearing and feeling oneself, and I do not mean that in a sexual context.

For example, have you ever taken time out to listen to your stomach, to feel your organs and how they work? Not a physical touch, but more internal. Have you ever sat and appreciated your eyes and how they are working well when there's nothing in them causing you to rub for dear life? Your back when it does not ache with pain or possible dislocation? What about your chest when it's not tight or aching with heartburn? How about your knees and how they are lubricated, allowing you to squat, run, and so on? Your overall physical body when everything is working as it should. Do you sit and mentally feel these things? Showing your body, and the things that make up your physical form, how much you appreciate them? Creating this mental space where you can be still, calm your energy and feel yourself—and the life that you are—is a must. To allow your body, whatever state it's in during this moment, to be, even if it's not how you want it to look.

Through meditation or "experiencing the gap," I've been able to understand just how much time is needed away from others. To be overly accessible to individuals, friends, and family, both physically and psychologically, can sometimes be a bit much. Constant chatting, constant movement. Sean Howard, a good friend of mine, tweeted, *"The most enjoyable people to be around are the ones who don't feel the need to disrupt moments of silence with useless conversation."* He was spot on with his writing. Further, it's been through this gap, that I've been able to grow my sense of self and understand the importance of solitude—this space of stillness where I've been able to connect the dots if you will.

> **Side Note: Jennifer B. Kahnweiler, author of Quiet Influence: The Introvert's Guide to Making a Difference, stated, "Not only does being intertwined with others deplete introverts' reserves of people energy, but it also takes them away from the physical and intellectual space where they do their best thinking. If you are an introvert, you know that you need to be alone to reflect and create." And I agree: introverts and extroverts alike understand that to hatch any great plan or idea they need a physical space where they can #GetShitDone.**

There are a few spaces that inspire me to clear my mind and restore my balance—all while maintaining my impressive physique. The gym is one of these spaces. Believe it or not, the gym is where I do my best thinking, where I can put two and two together, and I'm allowed to be in full control of who I am. My gym is a place that promotes me and encourages me to get better, to think clearly and became more aware. The more I sharpen my skills in the gym, the sharper I am in life, and in general (because, again, how you do one thing is how you do all things). From my physical training, I have become inspired to transform the other spaces I occupy into areas that encourages me to live happier and healthier.

In my bedroom, I've created a very calming environment that also doubles as an office space which inspires me to work when I'm ready. It's comfortable enough for me to sit still, while still encouraging me to **#GetShitDone**. Papers hanging from wall-to-wall, sketches, rough drafts of this book, and Post-it Notes that read, "You cannot fall off from who you genuinely are." I filled my space with a eucalyptus scent that clears congestion and uplifts my mood at the same time. I have two plants in my room that promote life and a bouquet of flowers on my desk that makes me happier at the sight of them.

At any full-time job I've had, I created my workstation to look the same: one big ball of motivation with positive quotes telling me to *"Just breathe,"* or *"Remember this will not last forever,"* and my favorite, *"This is what success looks like."* I'm reminded every day that this, too, will pass. I also have another plant sitting on my desk.

> **Side Note: Plants do a beautiful job of portraying life. They hold great conversations, and if you genuinely get to know them, you'll see they all have their own personalities. Mentally, I know if I can keep a plant alive, I am in balance. You know the saying, "Stop and smell the roses"? Well, I thought if I could stop and water my plants, then it must mean I wasn't overly consumed with my life situation and the things taking place outside of me. I am living in the now, and by watering and helping my plants grow, I am in some way doing the same for myself. To nurture and water them is to water and nurture me. If that makes sense?**

Furthermore, the impact of having a physical space that supports who you are helps you focus more on the things that matter, is a necessity. **#LifeGoals!** No matter whether I am home or at my day job, because I have the note that reads, *"This is what success looks like,"* I know I am right where I need to be, and that I'm doing what's needed. I am not missing out on anything! Even when I'm in the gym, that space helps me create new ideas for what I want to be a part of, and I know that the philosophy for WardBody is something that's very real. I am an Everyday Athlete, constructing my mind and body for my big playoff, and through the power of self- and social awareness I become.

Finally, the other spaces that help me live out my existence are the movie theater, the park, or a quiet coffee shop. All three of these places connect me closer to my source. I love nature, cool breezes on a summer day, the sounds of action films and the animation of any Marvel movie, and the aroma of coffee. These spaces help bring me closer to who I am, and once I leave them, I'm again refreshed, bright-eyed, and inspired.

Everything Connects

Despite how it may seem, the emotional, spiritual, and digital spaces we live in all have a powerful impact on parts of our lives. We can see evidence of this intertwined relationship if we look close enough. Take social media, for instance. On all my platforms, my following tends to be lower than my followers because social media is a space where if you see too much of something or read too much of something, it then makes its way into your actual life situation and soon becomes you.

For example, celebrity gossip I don't care about it, I don't want to discuss it, please don't ask my opinion. To me, it's all a gimmick. The stories we read and all that we know are ways to get us to buy into someone's celebrity or influence—it is not real life. Same goes for the news. The news is devoted to brainwashing. Consume too much of it, and soon you will not be able to think for yourself—and that's just what they want. Lastly, pornography it's everywhere, whether it's PornHub, Instagram, Twitter, or Myvdister all free of charge.

Further, I am not knocking what people are into, or what people do. Again, I have 0 degrees in how one should live their life; however, being overly consumed with these things helps shape who you are and your views on social issues and also your code of conduct. Be aware of this.

As an informed adult, I don't enjoy being in others' business, whether they are sharing it freely and willingly or if it's shared in the form of gossip. It has nothing to do with me, and I thoroughly enjoy not knowing. However, with social media, I enjoy looking at creators who create, singers who sing, and dancers who dance. I enjoy my cyberspaces to uplift and inspire me and occasionally wipe me out with laughter.

> *Athlete's Tip:* Disconnect and power down every weekend or every other weekend and get in touch with yourself. Go lie out in the park and allow nature to consume you. Free your mind as the wind passes through your hands and hair. How would your life look if the weight of your world were lifted from your shoulders, even if for one minute? How would you feel? Think these thoughts, feel these feelings, and focus on your breath. Mental and physical spaces are needed. Don't drive yourself crazy thinking you always need to be in the know or keep up; you don't.

Journal Entry

Dear Father God,

It's October 28th and I just got home from work at 11:22 pm. I'm very tired but must wake up tomorrow at 6:55 am to get ready for school. I honestly don't think there's an enough time in the day for me. I'm about to start my homework in a few, but I would just like to say thank you for making me who I am. I know many will not be able to handle what I have, and I just want to say thank you for making me who I am. I'm very strong and driven. I will never let anybody, or any obstacle hold me back from what I want and deserve in life. I will deal with what I must deal with, learning new patience and skills, for I respect my process in growing. I grow every day, but I certainly feel like my life has been backwards. The discipline I housed have been getting as a child I'm receiving and so many rules do not sit well with me. I have been on my own for years, taking care of myself, and for someone to think they will come into my life and treat me as if I'm a child.

I highly respect the favor of offering me a place to stay, but I'm no push over and I demand respect. I just ask of you, dear Father God, that you watch over me and guide me each and every day to get me where I will love to be and cherish the moments while getting there. You always send me through tests before the great outcome.

January 17, 2017
11:29 am

The 17th day of the new year, and I am feeling relaxed today. My workout was great; my breakfast was great. It's a very calming day.

However, I walked into work and was told the office manager was fired (Lisa). I am happy she is gone. Not that she doesn't need a job, but her energy was horrible to be around. And that just made me think about how jobs can let you go with no notice, yet they require a two-weeks' notice from you.

I don't know if I want to continue working here or if I want to look for another place to go. With WardBody on the up-and-up, I'm just thinking about my own company.

I would like to remain relaxed and chill today. But I am great, nonetheless.

Part Four
JUST BE QUIET SOMETIMES

Chapter 7
A GLIMPSE OF ENLIGHTENMENT!

> I'd like to offer something to help you; but here in the Zen school, we don't have a single thing!
>
> – Zen Master Ikkyu

Zen is a total state of focus that incorporates complete unity of body and mind. Zen involves dropping illusions and seeing things without the distortion created by your own thoughts. The term *Zen* stems from the Sanskrit word *dhyana*, which means "meditation" or "contemplation."

Zen can transform your sense of identity, resulting in far less stress and anxiety. One might say the essence of Zen consists of the realization that life is something like a great silly dream. And accepting all aspects of this dream—precisely as they are—at any given moment is the only way to liberate us from the unnecessary suffering that most of us inflict on ourselves.

In this chapter, you will read several Zen stories. Zen stories tend to be humorous, paradoxical, often puzzling, yet short and powerful. Along with each story is a *WardBody (WB) Lesson* and a self-reflecting question. Ponder these stories and emerge wiser and more self-aware than before.

#WARDBODY

Don't Worry

"For years, I've been listening to your lectures," said a student during the Q&A portion of a class given by Zen monk Suzuki Roshi. "But I just don't understand. Can you simplify it? Can you reduce Buddhism to one phrase?"

Everyone laughed; the Zen master joined.

"Everything changes," Suzuki said.

WB Lesson: Suffering will begin when you make evolution your opponent. You'll never have to worry for too long because everything comes to an end. Good or bad, enjoy the now and be prepared for what *is* to be what *was*.

Self-Reflection: Am I aware that what's today will not be tomorrow?

Perception

There was a farmer who had worked his crops for years. One day his horse ran away. Once his neighbors heard the news, they came to visit.

"Such bad luck," one said.

"Maybe," replied the farmer.

The next morning the farmer's horse returned and, with it, three other wild horses.

"How wonderful," one of the neighbors called out.

"Maybe," replied the old man.

The following day, the farmer's son tried to ride one of the wild horses. He was immediately thrown off and broke his leg. Again, the neighbors rushed over to offer their sympathy and comment on his bad luck.

"Maybe," the farmer answered.

The next day, military officials visited the village to draft young men into the army. Once the officials saw that the son's leg was in no condition for combat, they passed him by. The neighbors soon congratulated the farmer and his son on how well things had turned out.

"Maybe," replied the farmer.

WB Lesson: All things happen for a reason. Don't be so quick to judge events as good or bad; everything is in constant flux. Stay level-headed and avoid becoming too high with the highs and too low with the lows.

Self-Reflection: Do I truly understand that everything that has taken place in my existence all happened for a reason?

#WARDBODY

Before Anything Else...

Once a teacher and his student worked as a pair of acrobats. They performed daily on the streets to earn money for food.

Their act consisted of the teacher balancing a bamboo pole on his head while the little girl climbed slowly to the top. Once at the top, she remained there while the teacher walked along the ground.

One day the teacher said to the student, "Listen up: to prevent an accident, I will watch you, and you should watch me so that we can help each other maintain concentration and balance."

But the little girl was wise, so she answered, "Dear Master, I think it would be better for each of us to watch ourselves. To look after one self is to look after both of us. That way I am sure we will avoid any accidents and earn enough to eat."

WB Lesson: Before anything else, take care of yourself. Trying to save lives when your head is barely above the tide will result in more lives lost than saved.

Self-Reflection: Do I focus on myself enough? Am I too consumed with what others are doing with their time, and their selves?

A GLIMPSE OF ENLIGHTENMENT!

The Tea Warrior

There was once a famous tea master who lived on a mountain. His skill as a tea master was unsurpassed, and many came from all over to sit in his teahouse.

One day a short-tempered samurai burned his tongue on the master's tea. Enraged, he challenged the master to a duel.

As the warrior drew his weapon, the master turned to his apprentice.

"This duel is surely my end. I have done nothing but make tea my whole life. The teahouse is yours, my student."

"No, Master," the student cried out. "Take my sword. Face this warrior and raise your weapon in the same way you raise the teapot!"

The master walked into the courtyard, and the samurai rushed to attack.

The tea master closed his eyes and raised his weapon steadily toward heaven, with the same grace and strength he would command in the solemnest of tea rituals.

At this display of balance, the samurai panicked and thought, *This old man must be a master swordsman!*

The samurai fled the teahouse, never to return.

WB Lesson: How you do one thing is how you do all things. The thing that is going to protect you and bring you wealth is something you already do. Do only what you enjoy doing, and forever be rich.

Self-Reflection: What is it that I do that I genuinely enjoy doing?

#WARDBODY

Full Awareness

After several years of studying, a monk attained the rank of Zen teacher. After his advancement, he journeyed to visit his old Zen master.

When he walked into the house, the master greeted him and asked, "Tell me: Did you leave your umbrella on the porch?"

"Yes," the teacher replied.

"Tell me," the master continued, "did you leave your umbrella to the left or to the right of your sandals?"

The teacher realized he did not know the answer and that he had not yet attained full awareness. He stayed and studied with the master for several more years.

WB Lesson: It's not how much time you practice; it's about the quality of your practice.

Self-Reflection: Am I learning to recite or to genuinely know?

Perfection

A priest was informed that important guests were expected. Immediately, he began tending the garden. He removed weeds and pruned tree branches. He even combed the moss! Since it was autumn, the ground was covered with dry leaves, which the priest painstakingly arranged into neat mounds.

All the while, an old monk watched him. The priest finished with his labor of love. A look of satisfaction spread across his face. "Doesn't it look beautiful now?" he asked the monk.

"Indeed, it does," replied the monk, "but something's off. I'll fix it for you."

The old monk made his way slowly to a tree in the center of the garden, gripped its trunk, and shook it hard. Leaves scattered down, orange, russet, and brown. "There. That's better!

WB Lesson: Perfection "is"; it never "has to be."

Self-Reflection: Am I accepting of me, the real me? Do I own everything that is me?

#WARDBODY

The Warrior's Question

A warrior went to the Zen temple, seeking peace. On finding the master in meditation, the warrior was overcome with sadness. Though he knew he had fought bravely and justly for many years, he feared that he would never possess the grace and presence of the man before him.

"Why do I feel so inferior?" asked the warrior. "I know I have fought with honor, and I have nothing to be ashamed of. Yet seeing you just now, I feel my life has no significance whatsoever."

"Wait a while," said the master, smiling. "I will speak with you after I attend to the other visitors."

The warrior sat beneath a tree as visitors streamed through the temple, each one leaving the master with an expression of warmth on his face.

As night fell and the visitors dwindled, the warrior became distressed and asked the master, "Can you teach me now?"

The master nodded, and they walked to the rear, where the moon shone through a giant window, washing everything in white light.

"Do you see the moon, how beautiful it is?" said the master. "It will cross the sky and make way for the sun. The sun is much brighter and can illuminate clouds, mountains, and trees in ways the moon cannot. Yet have you ever heard the moon complain, 'Why don't I shine like the sun? Am I inferior?'"

"Of course not," said the warrior. "The sun and the moon are different; each has its own beauty. You cannot compare the two."

"So, you know your answer. We are two different people, each fighting in his own way for that which he believes and making it possible for the world to be a better place; the rest are mere appearances."

WB Lesson: Your style could be very similar to someone else's, as well as your aesthetic, your message, or your goal. But your purpose for existing in this world will be completely different. No one must fail for you to be great and to succeed. What truly matters is how you both are helping those in need.

Self-Reflection: Do I understand that no one else is me and that's my power?

#WARDBODY

What's the Difference?

A storm had just blown over, and hundreds of starfish had been washed up by the waves and begun to die in the intense sunlight. Ryokan, a Zen master, began picking up the starfish, one by one, and flinging them back into the sea.

A fisherman who'd been observing the Zen master came up to him and stated, "Every time there's a storm, this happens. Why do you do this? You can't save them all, so what difference does your attempt make?"

"It will make a difference—to this one," replied the Zen master, as he flung yet another starfish into the water.

WB Lesson: Your gestures and contributions to this world, society, and the people in it are never too big or too small. If you can plant a tree, and no one notices it, you've still planted a tree. You are never too good or not good enough to make a difference, and when it's truly from the heart, it never has to matter because you did it from love.

Self-Reflection: What starfish can I serve today?

A GLIMPSE OF ENLIGHTENMENT!

Zen in a Note

Once, a Japanese man, Kakua, visited China and became the first Japanese person to imbibe Zen teachings. He lived in a remote mountain area there and constantly meditated. When people accidentally encountered him, they asked him to preach. Kakua would utter a few words and move off to an even more inaccessible place in the mountains.

As Kakua's fame spread, the Japanese emperor heard about him. When Kakua returned to his home country, the emperor invited him to the court and requested that Kakua impart his teaching, both for the emperor's own illumination and for the benefit of the people of Japan.

Standing in front of the emperor, Kakua pulled out a flute from within his robe and blew a single note. He then bowed politely and walked out.

WB Lesson: Stop "trying," and simply "be." No one can teach you who you are.

Self-Reflection: Am I me, or am I pretending to be?

#WARDBODY

The Other Side

A monk, journeying home, reached the bank of a broad river. He could see no way to cross it. Standing there, he pondered for a while. *How can I get across?* he asked himself. No ideas occurred to him. Eventually, he gave up and was about to retrace his steps when he spotted a Zen teacher standing on the opposite bank. He yelled across to the older man, "Oh, Master, I am stranded here. Can you tell me how I may get across to the other side?"

The teacher thought for a few moments, looking up and down the river. He then shouted back, "My good fellow, you *are* on the other side!"

WB Lesson: Wherever you are in your journey right now, as you read this, is right where you need to be.

Self-Reflection: Am I aware that the grass is only greener because I decided to water it?

Chapter 8
THIS IS WARDBODY!

Your Mind

My sense of awareness and how I now think have not always been at this compacity, obviously. The way I retained information growing up, how I analyzed and processed it—in school, or within the jobs I had—would've been labeled "slow," or mentally retarded, in other words. Although I was very much so in a "normal" class with other "normal" kids, I could sense that I learned things a little differently than others. Certain information did not stick, and I needed someone to explain things to me a few times before I understood what was being taught or was asked of me to do. I am confident this has been due to my dyslexia.

> *Dyslexia* is a specific learning disability that is neurobiological in origin. It's characterized by difficulties with accurate and/or fluent word recognition and by poor spelling and decoding abilities. These difficulties typically result from a deficit in the phonological component of language that is often unexpected in relation to other

cognitive abilities and the provision of effective classroom instruction. Secondary consequences may include problems in reading comprehension and reduced reading experience that can impede growth of vocabulary and background knowledge.

– Dyslexia.org

    Education was never a top priority in my household while growing up. My advancement in academics fell by the wayside, along with everyone else's in my family, and I never understood just how bad my spelling and reading were until I had a friend, Whitney Brown, who mentioned I should focus more when writing text. Not knowing the risk factors of Dyslexia, I thought I was dyslexic because of my inability to finish out school and because I could never get the proper one-on-one time I knew I needed when in class. As a child, I struggled to pronounce big words and would get frustrated because I couldn't sound them out. Even with math, I physically cried one time because a problem was just too hard, and I did not get it. The same thing is now happening to one of my siblings, and it's eye-opening to me because I now know that I wasn't dumb or stupid.

    Moreover, I learned that school has nothing to do with having or developing dyslexia. Some of the actual risk factors are:

- A family history of dyslexia or other learning disabilities
- Premature birth or low birth weight
- Exposure during pregnancy to nicotine, drugs, alcohol, or infection that may alter brain development in the fetus

- Individual differences in the parts of the brain that enable reading

- Children who have dyslexia are at increased risk of having attention-deficit/hyperactivity disorder (ADHD), and vice versa. ADHD can cause difficulty in sustaining attention, as well as hyperactivity and impulsive behavior, which can make dyslexia harder to treat

I do think it's odd that we label people who learn differently than we do. We are all different, and we all process things differently, as it should be. Further, I struggled a lot because I had a hard time paying attention and would get super side-tracked by even the smallest thing; this stands true to this day. I learned I haven't been giving myself enough time to think things through and focus on the details, or even re-read something that wasn't 100% clear, which resulted in a ton of mistakes, even with the writing of this book.

My experience with writing this book, there's been times when I would get super sidetracked, and my mind would drift elsewhere, sometimes in five different directions. I would write for twenty minutes, and out of the blue, I'll begin doing something utterly unrelated to what I need to be doing. I'll start to clean, watch something on YouTube, or even run to the market, smack dab in the middle of a writing session, however, because I am aware of how my mind operates. Instead of forcing myself to do something, I've allowed my mind to wander. Listening to all of me has served me well. I guess you could say I got my mind right. Furthermore, this behavoir is a result of undoing and reprogramming myself with new habits.

#WARDBODY

> **Side Note: Did you know that most of the choices we make each day might feel like the product of well-considered decision making but are in fact habits? Did you also know that Daymond John—creator of FUBU, television host on Shark Tank, and the person who inspired me to write about my experience with dyslexia—is dyslexic? Did you know that Whoopi Goldberg, Jay Leno, Thomas Edison, and Walt Disney all identify with being dyslexic? I believe I am in good company.**

Learning how my mind works and how I processed information allowed me to take back my power—from people who thought they could use it against me, whether it be so-called friends or colleagues. I may have dyslexia, but I now know how to position myself and what's needed of me to get ahead. I also know that despite my diagnoses, I am one of the most creative, dedicated, self-driven, and fearless persons I know. I am no longer a victim or the butt of someone's joke because I know what's needed of me to win.

As basketball legend, Kareem Abdul-Jabbar said, "Your mind is what makes everything else work." What separates the Everyday Athlete from her competitors is her mentality and the way that she thinks. When asked, "How does one get in shape, or grow bigger blah blah blah? How do you do this or that?" My first answer is always, "Go visit AntoineWard. com because the answer should be there." However, at other times my answer is very generic—cliché, rather. I'll respond, "You have to get your mind right." Not only does it gets straight to the point, but also, it's a simple truth.

You will not begin to understand why you need to invest in things like amino acid or creatine or take precaution when eating certain foods if your mind is not right. The need to gain muscles, lose weight or vice versa will always stem from a superficial place: to either look better than, to look good for, or to look like. The average person wants to get in shape to look, never to feel, which is why many fitness journeys are over before they start.

The second you don't see results, you'll give up. You'll reminisce on how you spent a month in the gym, how you've spent all this money on organic food, yet don't see any results in your physical appearance. You won't being to acknowledge how well you feel, or how that kink in your neck is gone, and your anxiety has lessened. Fitness, just like success, requires you to do the same thing every single day for 365 days, and when you do hit that 365-day mark, you do it again for another 365 days, whether you see results or not!

There's no end to fitness. When you hit that goal weight, gained your muscle, lifted your cakes, or sculpted your arms, you must continue because now you must maintain your new gains. Fitness is consistency even when you don't feel like it; committing, even if there's snow on the ground, or raining falling from; failing, again and again, to see what you're about, proving to yourself what you can handle. Fitness is a feeling; it's not a look, and the moment you get your mind right, you'll understand this.

> *Athlete's Tip:* You must train your mind the way you train your body. Being in shape gets plenty of attention and for a good reason; however, being physically fit is an explicit representation of your mind. To see someone who's in shape is to know that person has fought an inner fight

or are fighting. Understand that fitness is your mental state of being. How are you wired?

Your Emotions

In addition to our mind, our emotions are absolute indicators of our vibrational content. In other words, they are the perfect reflection of our current point of attraction. They help us know when we are allowing or disallowing the fulfillment of our desires. We must pay attention.

Emotions are the most present and sometimes most painful forces in our lives, and we're driven by them daily. We sacrifice because we love; we fight when we feel threatened. It is without a doubt that our emotions dictate our actions, our thoughts, and sometimes our intentions. But we're all human, and as humans we all feel. The problem, however, is not that we feel; it is that we become so consumed with how we feel that we cannot think straight.

The most significant thing about me is that I am emotional, and not allowing my emotions to rule me has been the ultimate battle, in fact, learning how to control my feelings and separate what I do, from who I am was the last battle—with Self—that has allowed me to live happier and healthier.

"The key to winning was changing players habits."

- Tony Dungy,
Head coach of Tampa Bay Buccaneers

Allowing my feelings *to be*, was, and still is, an everyday practice. I have come to accept that shit happens, its life, more so, I have learned to let it. Resisting what is, is the gateway to being angry or any other negative emotion one may feel. Still, before understanding this, I couldn't see that at the root of every argument or debate was the need to prove a point; I am right, and you're wrong. That's all drama is.

Further, being disconnected from my source and not being honest with how I felt, I've granted others the opportunity to test me. I have allowed loved ones to choose for me and make me feel as if who I was wasn't enough. However, growing to understand the emotional being that is me, I no longer invite unwanted opinions into my space. Dropping my "prove a point" attitude has shown others that there is not and will not be an argument to win or lose, because I am not showing up to state a case. There's nothing I need to prove.

> **Side Note: Throughout this book, you may have noticed that I blame myself for many things that have happened to me. It is not blame, per se. I enjoy taking ownership of the roles I played, in addition to outcomes that have manifested in my life situation. Being able to see myself now and look back on who I may have been. I can see just how much power I've always had and how I was so afraid to stand in it, because of how others may view me.**

While accepting the fact that shit happens, you reading this, should know that before reaching a point of understanding your power there will be situations or people that must irritate you, stress you out, or disrespect you, all to help you define or create who you are not—full circle. In other words, you'll experience mistreatment, maybe you already have. You will be taken advantage of, or made out to be the bad guy, but in these moments, instead of taking on the role of the victim and indulging in the "he said, she said." Allow yourself the opportunity to become; focus on the lessons that are up for teaching. Calm your anger and think before doing. Realize that if it weren't for him, her, or them, you would still be that person that contradict him or herself. So, in hindsight give thanks to those who helped you reveal you, to yourself.

Blinded to the fact that not making a choice was, indeed, making a choice, I couldn't see how not choosing to leave a space, or someone behind was letting that person or thing, physiologically, know how he or she could treat me. By not taking ownership of ourselves, we permit those who mistreat us. *"The ability to choose cannot be taken away or given away—it can only be forgotten,"* said Greg Mckeown, author of Essentialism: The Disciplined Pursuit of Less. Through our emotions and how we feel for others, we forget that we can choose and that we have options.

Our emotions tell us when we're either allowing or resisting what *is*. The feelings of joy, passion, and enthusiasm are all signs that you are living in what many calls the now. You are at peace with what is happening. You're allowing the greatness that is to be. For example, your wedding day, your graduation, or maybe when you're having sex, you are allowing yourself to be within those moments, in that space, and it feels fantastic. Nothing about you is resisting walking down the aisle or across the stage to collect your diploma. The complete opposite happens when you are depressed or stressed out. These emotions indicate that you are resisting what *is*. Maybe someone stole your car, or you just found out JJ is entertaining others while dating you, or perhaps you were recently terminated.

Further, when stuff like this happens, it is in our nature, as beings, to panic. We drop the "now," and focus on the future because we no longer know what's going to happen, it's unknown. You knew how you were going to get to work tomorrow, but now your car is gone. You believed a relationship was in the process, yet now, you're confused. However, within moments of panic, you should know that you are still in control of your well-being. Although these may seem like great examples to worry or stress over, they aren't. Simply let be, and you'll soon see why.

The Universe has a funny way of showing us what we need to let go of to prosper. There's no such thing as a loss; only those who want to be down and out will be. If we forever allow what *is* to *be*, there will be no worry—*no hakuna matata!*

Surrender and become!.

In My Feelings...

Back in 2013, I'd begun getting to know this guy. We seemed very compatible; however, he lived in Atlanta, and I was living in Baltimore, soon to reside in New York. During our first phone conversation, I remember feeling like I couldn't believe I had so much in common with someone, from both of us being juniors to wearing the same color of contacts in high school, and we both struggled with speaking up for ourselves. Our entire conversation went, "OMG, me, too." After a few months of us getting to know each other, I had a feeling that one day this guy would make me happy and do me the honor of being my first-ever boyfriend.

Come that September, I purchased a round-trip ticket to see him for the first time, and after spending the first night with him, I was sold. It was a great experience, although I could sense some things were off, it didn't matter because I was head over heels for this boy. The longer we grew to know each other, the more I began to project myself onto him. However, I ignored my intuition and the fact that none of his friends, not even his "best friend," knew about me or why I'd come to Atlanta, which was odd, but I did not speak or make mention of this. I kept quiet about it and didn't mentally unpack this until I made it back home.

In October 2013, we called it quits. Well, he called it quits. My possessiveness grew, and I admit it was not pretty. I was thinking about weddings and kids. I became overly protective, and at the same time, I was very insecure, so I nagged a lot. I even considered moving to his hometown so that we could be together. My emotions got so out of hand, and I was so out of touch with myself, but I'd never met someone who made me feel the way I felt about him, this passion that I had. Moreover, I felt deeply for him and wanted to own him because that's what I thought love was when in fact, I was simply infatuated with this guy, and I was about to make a ton of permanent decisions due to this emotion.

Over time, I became very toxic and would say anything to get a reaction out of him. One day as we texted, I said something to piss him off, and he wrote back, "Sometimes you just need to shut the fuck up." Oddly enough, I agreed. It was clear that I wasn't emotionally mature or equipped to be in this relationship, but there was something about our connection because, come January 2015, we were back on. When we decided to get to know each other again, he mentioned to me that one of his close friends—the best friend that hung out with us when I visited ATL back in 2013—wanted to be more than just friends and the friend made a pass at him. Now, I'd known something was up, I just couldn't put my finger on what it was, but this time around I was not the same person. As he told me, I replied that I knew something was going on from the way he was moving; his energy was funny.

Without thinking, I allowed him to be the assertive one in the relationship, and I fell victim to the roles that gay society said we had to play in our relations, in other words, I allowed him to be the top and me the bottom. As an adult, I now know that dominating or being submissive does not make you either (a top) or (a bottom), but that's what our relationship signified. When we first met, he had a more dominant exterior, and I'd agreed, without words, to play that role for him. I led with being submissive in this relationship, and I am not a submissive person, and my toxic behavior was me fighting to reclaim myself and take back all that I'd given him.

However, in 2015, I was none of whom I used to be. I had grown. It became clear that although I felt what I felt for him I was thinking more logically about our situation. I began to understand the reason why he couldn't invest much in me and why I lashed out because of it. I learned that he couldn't invest in me because he didn't know how to invest in himself. He didn't know where he was going in his life, let alone trying to create or and experience life with me. I was expecting—hoping, wishing—to be number one in this man's life when he wasn't number one in his own life.

December 2015, I reached my breaking point within our relationship and grew tired of trying to prove to myself that I was a good man to be with or force myself to be a part of someone's life who clearly did not want me. There came a time where the opportunity to speak about being partners, I felt, was on the table. However, a few weeks before our planned vacation a situation happened with his job, causing him to lose his spot on this vacation, which then resulted in our relationship being put on hold.

Further, as I laid out in Cozumel, Mexico alongside my good friend Whitney, I concluded that I no longer wanted Us. I grew tired of being constantly let down because someone was unsure about himself and where he was going in life. I got tired of trying to ride for someone who I felt was going in circles. I'd learned a great deal from our situation. I was uninspired.

Come January 2016—new me, who dis?

> *Athlete's Tip:* Our emotions influence the way we think and the way we behave. So, it's crucial that we become aware of how our emotional reactivity can change our perception and, ultimately, our behavior. Our emotions are best met with a sense of moderation and logical perspective. I am not suggesting that anyone become cold-hearted or become a "savage"—as the kids say. However, I am encouraging you to become more aware of what you feel and not to make any rational decisions that you could later regret. Your mind and your emotions go together. As an empathetic person who feels things on a deep level, I advise that if you feel you cannot control your feelings, spend some time alone and bean to undo.

Your Outcome

Control!
    Self-control is your outcome!
Power!
    Power is your outcome!
Love!
    Love is your outcome!

THIS IS WARDBODY!

If there is anything, I would like for you to take away from this book, it's to be more in tune with Self. You cannot save anyone if you have not saved yourself. There will be no real bonding or connection to and from another if you have not gotten to know who you are. You will not begin to experience real love if you do not love you! We must make it our business to become more self-, socially aware.

While this book does—what I believe is—a great job at outlining what it means to be an Everyday Athlete and explains how to live both happier and healthier, it has an even more critical message. This book offers you an opportunity to connect with yourself, both physically and psychologically. Awarding yourself the chance to know you, and who you truly are, is the only thing I would like to offer you, followed by undoing, questioning, and thinking freely.

After reading this book, I would like for you to understand that greatness isn't something you must run after; it's already in you. You are already great, but great at what? That's the goal here. You must act on the events that have transpired in your life situation. Pain, misfortune, and depression, we are given these things for a reason, and it's time we find out what we need to apply these experiences—these lessons too.

Again, you do not need permission to do what you want to do. Life is honestly but a dream, and it's indeed what you make it. Appreciate who you are, your mistakes, and where you are within this very moment as you wrap up this book. Remember that you can never fail if you do not stop moving and know that life does not have to be lived in luxury to be meaningful or lived with a purpose. Your outcome is for you to realize, "I am love, and I am life." Your outcome is to know the things you seek you already are. Realize that you are power; you are the creator. Once aware of this, you can begin to awaken and soon walk in your life's purpose.

Even if you don't have everything you want, know that you have everything you need. You know and understand that stuff and titles do not make you; you make them. Your outcome is being your person and aware of your mind and how you think, what you feel, and getting in the habit of listening to your inner self. Which then promotes confidence, and inner joy and enhance your presence. Others will begin to feel you, the real you. "It's just something about him"

The world is going to move; allow it. Don't try to force yourself into cramped spaces; don't shrink because of adversity. Do you feel out of place? Good! Flow with that.

Your outcome is self-perseverance.

I created WardBody not to inspire, but to live. With this book, for example, where you see a product, I see a moment in time where I merely lived. This book is an example of me experiencing and experimenting with life. I finally understand just why I've been through so much in my life; I finally get why things have happened for me. This whole time, through misfortunes and unhappiness, I have been winning, silently, and I didn't realize it until I summarized my life situations into an eight-chapter book. The stories and lessons in this book were given to me to share with you all, which is also confirmation that you can come from nothing and still win! You can go through hell and still get up and move on. You can write your own will.

Your outcome is self-sufficiency.

When purchasing this book, did you think you were going to read about how eating right and going to the gym will help you live happier and healthier? Fitness is much broader than going to the gym and eating right. Again, fitness is how you think. It's how you take moments of suffering and use them as coal to light a fire in you, or as moments of education, to learn. Fitness is how honest you are with yourself. From this moment on, stop lying to yourself. The gym may not be for you. Maybe it's boxing; perhaps it's Pilates or Zumba, maybe even CrossFit? Go find out! Who are you? What do you like? What do you enjoy? Stop going out of your way trying to appeal to a group of individuals for public acceptance. Fold into who you already are and go with that; build on that.

Your outcome is self-fertilization.

When we are not aware as to what we are living for nothing in our life will last—not our diets, our meal planning, our daily gym routine, or our relationships. Nothing will stand the test of time if we are not aware as to why what is, *is*!

It's like working a dead-end job. On your first day, the excitement will be there. "Yes, I have arrived," you tell yourself. Then comes month three or six, and the thrill is gone, you're bored, and you are no longer excited about what is. You only show up to get a check and go home. Soon, if you don't quit, you'll get laid off. Trust me! Within the last four years, I've either been fired or let go from five different jobs—and by the time you read this, I'll probably be fired from job six, but it's okay, this is what success looks like.

It would be best if you understand your purpose for all that you do. What is the highest contribution you can make to help move the culture forward? What gifts do you have that can help others? What do you need to start, or be a part of? What are you supposed to help build? Who are you supposed to assist? With every failed attempt at working in Corporate America and being aware of every situation I've ever been in, within a company, I know what I am supposed to do and just why I am here.

When we don't know or aren't aware of our purpose, we began doing *"just because"* shit. Meaning, we go out and drink every weekend, just because it's something to do, or we entertain those we do, with no real expectation of making him or her our Boyfriend or Girlfriend because we aren't aware of what we want. There is no real value in *just because* shit. You do it, just because. Not understanding your purpose, you won't hit the gym consistently or invest in organic or gluten-free goods because you don't feel it serves a purpose in your life, because, you don't know what your purpose is. You won't see the benefits, and the *take away* from certain things and people; certain jobs because you aren't aware as to why these things are happening to you. You'll continue to live the life that you do and conjure up excuses to avoid doing *the work*.

Your outcome is self-awareness.

To Wrap This Up...

Being inspired by the life that has chosen me, I've decided to write about the actual things that fitness is built upon: loss, confusion, depression, love. These are the reason why one should eat healthily, and exercise daily, as opposed to wanting a big butt or bigger arms.

I take care myself because I love myself because I enjoy how running makes me feel. I am more confident after weight training, and I appreciate myself a little more after a HIIT session. Through constructing Self, I understand that I am only human and while there's only but so much I can take, there is nothing I cannot do or get through if my heart and my mind are in the right place. However, this book is more profound than fitness, and it was in my nature to share with you how deep a healthier and happier lifestyle is to me and let you in on my Why.

The gym isn't my life, nor is investing in organic goods and chemically free products. These things are additions to my life, for me, myself. I am life. These things help me live out my purpose, which is to build a new earth, by helping you awaken your life's purpose through the power of self and social awareness.

I, Antoine Ward, believe real life tends to be experienced once one understands and are aware of what we're living for.

Your outcome is self-efficacy.

— WARD

Journal Entry

October 7, 2013
9:36 pm

I feel like I'm about to get my heart broke. Why does this always happen to me? I try being loyal and kind to people, I really do. I always get this feeling that I'm more into whomever I'm dealing with—I like them more than they like me. And it's not a great feeling. But I'm not trying to play games with my heart. If I feel the way I do, why can't I show it? Why can't I express it? Why do I have to hold something back that's so real and genuine about myself? Why can't anyone appreciate what I feel for them? Why do my feelings get taken for granted? Over the years, I've put my heart on the line to get nothing back in return. I can't help that about myself, that I fall the way I do, and always have people telling me I need to change that about myself. Why do I become so upset over what didn't work out and let it make me into someone who doesn't want to love again? Someone who doesn't want everything he dreamt of when it comes to love? I'm not going to let anyone ruin the fact that I love, love. It's one of the greatest things about me. I care for others and I'm there, and if no one wants that in their life, that is fine with me. Someone will come along and love everything about me and what I have to offer.

June 30, 2017
7:19 am

Today, I feel amazing as I fly back to Mexico City to get back to NYC. My birthday was a total success, aside from the emotions I displayed yesterday, but even in that moment, I was still happy.

In life I learned that it is all up to me, to make me happy. To be true, to make myself and my life, the work of art I want it to be. I also learned that you must be careful who you choose to enter your life. Family, friends, coworkers, boyfriends, girlfriends. Because you must take full responsibility for the energy they bring. I learned I'm the happiest when I'm alone because there's nothing and no one that can ruin that. Like little things, for example getting to the airport when I want. Rolling in a group, other people will want to be on their time, and I want to be on mine. I like to be able to do everything I want, when I want to do it, and not have to answer to anyone. It's because of my childhood; this I have learned and figured things out about my childhood and it's helping me out a lot. I feel like I figured out the language of the universe. Like I get it now.

And I feel so rich because of it. I sat yesterday just thinking about everything, as I always do, and I just know what I feel about myself and who I'm supposed to be in life is real.

I know my purpose is to create, to help, to heal, and to encourage, and add value to people's lives. Everyone I have ever met I feel I've done that for them, without evening knowing that's what I was doing. My mom was doing the same thing. And I think it's my purpose. My mother has blessed me with caring, and I am proud and thankful to take it on.

ACKNOWLEDGEMENTS

Thank you to my loved ones for putting up with my inconsistency as I write this book.

To Whitney Brown, my dear friend, who in many ways has helped me throughout my journey, who has shown great support in countless ways, and who have literally listened to every single theory I could come up with for this book. Never annoyed when I said, "I wrote that in my book" You are one of the first persons to know what it means to live a WardBody lifestyle and to be an Everyday Athlete.

To the special guy in my life, during the time of editing this book, thank you for offering me an opportunity to live and experience moments of fun when I desperately needed it. Thank you for distracting me from the drama that has taken place in my life, and being a support system for me during the past year and a half. Lastly, thank you for trying your best to be what I needed.

To Sean Howard, who has allowed me to call on him in my time of need, who have stuck by and helped develop the image of what living happier and healthier looks like to me. Thank you for your solid ear and your honest feedback.

To my family and the men and women who have

walked in and out of my life, had it not been for you I would not be who I am today. Thank you for doing the best that you could and allowing me to see that I can do more. Thank you for love, harassment me, and disrespect. I can humbly and genuinely admit I appreciate it.

    Lastly, I want to thank myself. Antoine Ward, thank you for continually moving on. Even when you've felt what you were doing wouldn't make a difference. Thank you for respecting and taken great care of yourself. Thank you for having morals, and for learning and understanding that you deserve more, and that you are deserving. Thank you for knowing that there's so much more to life and that you can own it if you want. Thank you for not turning to drugs. Thank you for showing love and support and always being the bigger person when I know you would much rather give people what they've given you. Thank you for taking ownership of yourself, for loving who you are, and believing in what you do.

    You have come so far, and I am so proud of you. Continue to be a man of your word, cherish your mind and body, and never ever give up!

    I love you,

– Ward

ABOUT THE AUTHOR

I have no special talents. I am only passionately curious.

- Albert Einstein

Antoine Ward Jr. is nothing and no one. Ward has turned his passion for fitness and his will to excel into an active lifestyle Brand–WardBody. A lifestyle he take's pride in saying he lives. This book is Antoine's first. He Lives in New York.

www.ingramcontent.com/pod-product-compliance
Lightning Source LLC
Chambersburg PA
CBHW030322080526
44584CB00012B/665